D1544818

THE NEW BRITISH POETS

By Kenneth Rexroth

POETRY

In What Hour
The Phoenix and The Tortoise
The Signature of All Things

EDITOR

Selected Poems of D. H. Lawrence
California Poets

The New British Poets

AN ANTHOLOGY

EDITED BY

KENNETH REXROTH

A NEW DIRECTIONS BOOK

ACKNOWLEDGMENTS

For permission to reprint the poems appearing in this volume acknowledgments are due to the following publishers and periodicals, both British and American:

Jonathan Cape Ltd., *Circle, Contemporary Poetry & Prose, The Cornhill,* Andrew Dakers Ltd., Doubleday & Co., *The Dublin Magazine,* Dutton, Faber & Faber, *Focus,* The Fortune Press, The Grey Walls Press, The Hogarth Press, Henry Holt & Co., *Horizon, Illiterati,* Alfred Knopf, *Leaven,* John Lehmann Ltd., *Life & Letters, The Listener, The London Mercury,* The Macmillan Co., William McClellan, *New Road, New Verse,* The Oxford University Press, *Poetry Chicago, Poetry Folios, Poetry London, Poetry Quarterly, Poetry Scotland,* Random House, George Routledge Ltd., Martin Secker & Warburg, The Seizin Press, *Time & Tide, Transformation,* The Viking Press.

ALL RIGHTS RESERVED

821
R45

PRINTED IN ITALY
BY THE OFFICINE TIPOGRAFICHE A. MONDADORI AT VERONA

AS EVER – TO MY WIFE

MARIE

AND TO MY FRIEND

JIM LAUGHLIN

THE POETS

INTRODUCTION

IN the early years of the world economic crisis, a group of young British poets came into great prominence both in England and America. From 1932 to 1937 they spoke for a world on the eve of disaster. Their success was tremendous. Everyone knows their names: W. H. Auden, Stephen Spender, C. Day Lewis, Louis MacNeice, and their friends and associates. In 1937 a change of taste, a reaction, set in. It was inconspicuous at first, but with the onset of universal war, most of the poetry being written in England was of a new and different kind. At the least it was a new manner, at the best it was a new vision. Most of its adherents and practitioners call themselves Romantics. It is the purpose of this collection to represent the work of those British poets who have come to prominence since 1937 as extensively as possible. It is not a Romantic collection, in the sense of being weighted in favor of that tendency. I have included as wide a representation as I could of the English poets who were born during or after 1908, that is, who will be forty or under on the publication of this book. In addition, I have tried to give some picture of the extremely active Scottish literary renascence, without regard to age.

Looking back, it seems today that the Auden circle was more a merchandizing co-operative than a literary school. Certainly its members have drifted far apart. Auden himself is now an American citizen. His influence in England is slight. To use Ossietsky's phrase, his voice sounded hollow across a frontier and ocean to his juniors who were sitting out the London blitz. His sympathy with Marxism, never too well grounded, has vanished and he has almost forgotten his special mythology, the Public Schoolboy, the garden party, the country house; and with Mr. Gerald Heard, sometime science popularizer for the B. B. C., he has become the spokesman for a peculiarly American, Hollywoodweary religiosity. Cecil Day Lewis, like Louis Aragon and others of that kidney, has become a conventional if not a popular writer. Louis MacNeice is trying desperately to cure himself of the bad habits of his youth, the flat, "wise," pedestrian writing that earned him the label of the perfect urban poet. Minor figures in the group, like Rex Warner, have taken to novels, or disappeared, or both.

Only Stephen Spender has made a transition into the new period, and for reasons I shall discuss later, this has not been difficult for him. Contemporary with the Auden circle, more or less, were two other groups, not as well known in America, but, in their day, very influential in England: the Cambridge metaphysicals, and the objectivists who contributed to *New Verse*.

Auden's friends were mostly Oxonians. At Cambridge a group grew up around William Empson, the author of *Seven Types of Ambiguity*, which included Charles Madge, Richard Eberhart and Kathleen Raine. There was something peculiarly American about them, something a little barbarous and Poe-esque. The Auden circle were very British, and seemed to believe that poetry could best be written from an attitude, a very British attitude exemplified by Byron's satires, Prior, Peacock, Clough, Lear, Benson, Calverly, Belloc, and the authors of the best dirty limericks. At utilitarian Cambridge, on the other hand, there is more than a suspicion that they believed that you could write poetry from a formula, and that, if you searched hard enough and with scientific methods learned from Ogden and Richards, you were sure to find the formula, what with all our modern advantages. Empson's own poetry, when it is "ambiguous," is like nothing so much as something vast built with an Erector set, complex, insensitive and dispassionate. At his best he actually resembles Auden when he is at his best, simple, wistful, and conscience ridden—again, not unlike Arthur Hugh Clough. In the medium he and his group tried to develop, the American metaphysicals fostered by John Crowe Ransom are incomparably better. It is significant that the American poet, Richard Eberhart, who was at Cambridge for a while, is the best poet to have come under Empson's influence. He, certainly, does not believe that it is possible to discover a recipe for writing like John Donne. Another exception is Kathleen Raine, the youngest of the group, who has moved on and grown and is one of the leading poets of the new period.

Geoffrey Grigson, the editor of *New Verse*, is usually looked on as the founder and leader of British Objectivism, which needs careful distinction from the American school of the same name. American Objectivism, of which I happened to be an unwilling leader, took off from William Carlos Williams, Pound, the Stein of *Tender Buttons*, Yvor Winters' early work, and a variety of French writers — Cendrars, Apollinaire, Cocteau, MacOrlan, Deltiel, Soupault, and certain phases of Aragon, Tzara and Eluard. I suppose it could be called the last gasp of literary cubism. Like cubism, it depended far more on an entranced sense of hyper-reality, a sort of hallucination of fact, than on its fancied objectivity. There was nothing of this in British Objectivism, neither the learning, nor the revolt, nor the international connections, nor the rarefied aesthetics. They just put it down as it came. The results are often startling. It is difficult to understand, sometimes, what Grigson himself thought he was getting at — with his inventories of seascapes and city streets — one expects to find a notice of a Sheriff's Sale at the end of the poem. At its best this tendency produced writing somewhat like MacNeice's flattest exercises but with more things in it. Constituting as it did a technique of discretion and suppression, the flat, tightly cemented armor plate of stuff sometimes accumulated quite a head of steam underneath. Kenneth Allott and Bernard Smith, for instance, really have a lot of banked fire in them. Grigson did teach many to write simply, lucidly, without posturing or trickery, which is all to the good. His influence on younger men like Ruthven Todd has been nothing but salutary.

Julian Symons' *Twentieth Century Verse* was another focus for tendencies indistinguishable from the Auden circle, but which included a somewhat different set of people. Symons himself, and Roy Fuller — both of whom have changed considerably since those days — are the most important members of this group.

Fuller is one poet to whom the term classical can be applied with justice. His work has a clarity, order, and succinctness which is exceptional in present day England. At the same time he is personally involved in his expression, in the same way as the best Romantic poets.

Independent of all this, there was lightning in the mountains to the North — Hugh Macdiarmid and the Scottish Renascence, a completely separate phenomenon in, for cultural purposes at least, a separate country. It is surprising how little influence the work of a major poet and hyperactive publicist like Macdiarmid has had in England.

In 1948, the majority of British poets under forty consider themselves Romantics, and look on the preceding period as one of Classicism. The movement, which has certainly been a revolution, and which has very nearly swept all before it, is known officially as Romanticism. I realize that everybody knows what Romanticism and Classicism mean, but I am very suspicious of the words. They did not come into existence until well on in the Romantic period. Horace and Virgil did not look on Catullus as a Romantic. I think it is as misleading to describe Auden as a Classicist as it is so to describe Byron. It is better to try and find out what happened.

On the eve of the second war, the intellectual world generally was still dominated by the gospel of artistic impersonality, inherited from the nineteenth century "scientific," "exact aesthetic," and the opposed cult of artistic irresponsibility, "Art for Art's Sake." Mallarmé, Valéry, Cubism, much Marxism, the dubious "Thomism" of M. Maritain, T.S. Eliot, Laura Riding, Robert Graves, I.A.Richards, most Surrealists — it was almost universally taught and believed that the work of art was not communicative, was not "about anything." Instead, it should be approached empirically, from a utilitarian basis, as an object existing in its own right, a sort of machine for precipitating an "aesthetic experience." The artist's job was to be a consummate craftsman, to construct his machine so that it would go off at just the right time in the spectator's face, and have just exactly the intended effects. However, like the manufacturers of most time bombs and infernal machines, he should exercise the greatest caution not to leave any fingerprints in the machinery. As nearly as possible, the work of art should seem to be a sort of minor Act of God, a sublime, impersonal accident. The job of the critic, who preferred to be called an aesthetician, was to pick up the pieces and reconstruct the machine, so that other machines like it could be made, and so that the spectator would have a clinical knowledge of what was expected of him the next time one went off. If there were any telltale fingerprints around, they were ignored with a nervous little laugh as the business of vulgar detectives. This theory completely dominated European art for almost half a century. There is only one trouble with it, and that is that it isn't true. There are no such works of art. The painting of Picasso, or even Mondrian, the sculpture of Brancusi, the poetry of Eliot or Valéry, the music of Stravinsky, they are all intensely personal. In fact, they are amongst the most personal works of art in the history of culture.

I believe that this rigorous rationalism, this supression of all acknow-ledgement of personality, feeling, intuition, the denial of communi-cation and of the existence of emotion, is part of the general sickness of the world, the Romantic Agony, the splitting of the modern personality, the attempt to divorce the brain from the rest of the nervous system. Reason and emotion, Nell Gwynne and Cromwell, puritanism and libertinism, stare in each other's eyes across the mind of modern, especially modern British and American, man. Where-ever a poet of major talent has tried to hide himself behind his reason as though it were some abstract, geometrical facade, he has only succeeded in further torturing and exposing his personality. Thus the abiding unity in the work of Valéry is not his sweated Racine surface, but his specialized sensibility, his pained fastidiousness, and his special hell. Minor talents flourish under the encouragement of neo-classic fashions only because there are always handy-men about with nothing to hide and nothing to expose.

So with British poetry of the first years of the world crisis. All these carefully cultivated echoes of Mother Goose, the Anti-Jacobin, Ed-ward Lear, Cole Porter, W. S. Gilbert, Anglo-Saxon riddles, The Face On The Bar Room Floor, were well enough understood in America as masks, like the masks in the paintings of Max Beckman, hiding something very unhappy if not nasty. That was precisely the point. By speaking slowly and distinctly in a quiet voice, with com-mon accents, one might get the patient to pay attention. The most effective warning of onrushing disaster is presumed to be the one spoken with the minimum of affect. Then too, it is apparent that the constant theme of Auden's poetry, at least, is: "I am just as sick, if not a little sicker, than thee." The trouble was that the idiom, this strange high-brow music-hall jargon, was too artificial, too dis-honest as speech, to wear well. It was a carefully learned bedside manner, a kind of dialect verse; and nothing is more distressing than poor dialect verse once it has gone out of date. W. H. Auden's *New Year's Letter*, the worst book he has written and one of the worst books of our time, reminds me of nothing so much as J. V. Weaver's *In American*, or James Whitcomb Riley. It is just the unsuccessful recording of the patois of a different social level. As a matter of fact, Auden has consistently preached personal involvement; personal responsibility — but his language has slipped deeper and deeper into his own special literary cocktailese, it has grown harder and harder to believe him. He never seems, himself, to be really involved, to ever practice what he preaches. His Chinese, Iceland and Spanish books have a shallow, flippant impersonality about them which makes very unpleasant reading. Sometimes this all falls away, as in the September 1939 poem and "Human on my faithless arm;" again and again in Auden there is a profoundly moving, despairing, nightbound, personal cry, and then back again comes the old snide bright jargon. I think the reaction against him is much less than the reactors imagine. Most of them are acting on the imperatives of his best poems, and few of them have escaped from his worst fault — a peculiar rhetorical imprecision of language, a tendency to talk in terms of secondary reference instead of presentational immediacy, which is the besetting sin of most British verse with the exceptions of D.H. Lawrence, Ford Maddox Ford and Herbert Read.

However much the practice of Auden himself may have been misunderstood, and however little it was lived up to, there is no doubt that there did exist in England a well established cult of impersonality, ultimately of artistic irresponsibility, unchallenged until the eve of the war. I think it was the events of the years 1935-36-37, more than any literary factors, which forced the issue of communication, the person to person responsibility of artistic creation, back into prominence.

Along with this aesthetics went, as everyone knows, a political program, or at least attitude — Marxism or what passed for Marxism — that is, a greater or less degree of sympathy and identification with the maneuvers of Russian foreign policy. One would think that revolutionary politics and aesthetic impersonalism would be contradictory, but Bolshevism is precisely an anti-personal, anti-humane revolution. The whole point of Marxism is that the millenium occurs by accident, everything gets worse and worse until suddenly we are living in the best of all possible worlds. Furthermore, the artists in uniform of Bolshevik culture have no place for Blakes, Shelleys and Lawrences in their ranks. The job of the artist is to turn out, exactly as an American advertising copy writer, the most persuasive devices possible. The content is supplied by the client, in this case, the Russian Bureaucracy. This led to a lot of agonized theorizing about the relation of form and content amongst the more honest fellow travellers. This is a childish question, which answers itself, and it was pitiful to see men of intelligence fretting themselves over a pseudo problem which had never before appeared in serious criticism or aesthetics. The reason being, of course, that humane men had never before got themselves in such a predicament. Today, literary Marxism has vanished in England, but it would be very unwise to underestimate its importance. At one time it was all-powerful.

The attempted Marxization of literature had effects not unlike the forced collectivization of agriculture in Russia. People noticed the baby going down the drain with the bath. Poetry was ceasing to be about anything more important than sociological formulae. Just at this time the Spanish War broke out. Then, after the first flush of enthusiasm had been cultivated carefully by the Popular Front, came the Moscow Trials, like a year-long bludgeoning of the naked heart, and, following the Trials, the manifest butchery of the Spanish Revolution for the exigencies of Russian foreign policy.

The terror and betrayal of those years seem to have had a far more profound effect over there. In America the intellectual Left took it all pretty much in stride. It seemed, from the distance of Hollywood or 57th Street at least, no worse than Al Capone's antics, and it was for the worthiest of objects, the eventual brotherhood of man. The humane tradition did not die so easily in England. British opinion was outraged, and revolted violently. Then too, most British observers in Spain were at least partially independent of the Stalinists and their whiskey-soaked, hairy-chested journalists who looked on the Spanish War as a somewhat more thrilling bull fight. The Independent

Labor Party had a group there, naturally in sympathy with the most persecuted Spanish group, the P.O.U.M., there were many Labor Party people, and even the British Stalinists were controlled by their political commissars only with difficulty. This is all important. I believe that Spain, more than the Trials, the Pact, or even the War itself, marked the climacteric in British intellectual life, and I have never spoken or corresponded with anyone who did not agree with me. The moral earnestness and personal integrity which have been supposed to be typically British virtues reasserted themselves decidedly, even in the ranks of those who should have recovered from such petty bourgeois deviations. It is precisely these characteristics which were to be sought and cultivated deliberately in the ensuing period, and it is a moral quality, rather than a literary theory, which marks the New Romanticism.

After the Spanish War it is almost as though literary England withdrew in a sort of uneasy, wounded isolation from European letters. There was a brief, half-hearted attempt to popularize Surrealism. Herbert Read talked about it and wrote about it. There were Surrealist magazines and galleries. David Gascoyne, then a very young man, became its most enthusiastic spokesman and exponent. British Surrealism never fell into the idle silliness of male hair dressers and parfumistes, like its American counterpart, but it never took on. Since it had already died at its source — the best French Surrealists had long since become Stalinists — the British, closer to France than the Americans, realized that Breton's little remant were as isolated, as furious, and as meaningless, as their political bedfellows, the Trotskyites.

Then too, if Marxism was not the answer, the vulgar Freudianism mixed with Old Bolshevik intransigeance of Surrealism was not the answer either. Both were patently mechanistic, anti-personal interpretations of the human situation. Further, as the crisis of Western culture deepened, it was obvious that Surrealism was empirically a failure. It simply could not do what it proposed to do. It was unable to live up to its very rash promises. A few painstakingly constructed exercises in "free association" written in the monotonous argot of the Freudian couch were no match for the actual nightmares come true that went on in the newspapers. Certainly such pathetic toys were never going to "revolutionize the human sensibility as such," in the brave words of André Breton. In fact, they rapidly degenerated into the sterile clichés of a dying popular fad, about as revolutionary as "knock, knock," Pee-Wee Golf, and "Confucius say," their somewhat more or less vulgar contemporaries.

In the meantime, independent of programs and manifestos, changes were taking place in the practice of poetry. Even the more astute early reviewers of the work of Stephen Spender had noticed that there really wasn't much in common between him and the rest of the Auden circle. Those who compared him to Shelley were not far wrong. To avoid the words Classic and Romantic, if Auden and Day Lewis and MacNeice were primarily constructive artists, Spender was primarily an expressive one. Further, he was much more interested in himself and his own integration into the world than in any political solution. Even his politics was exceptional. He was never seduced by the attractively disguised blandishments of Stalinism. It is no accident that he wrote, not about the battles of the Popular Front, so carefully disciplined by the tommy-guns of the G.P.U., but about the lonely and hopeless struggle of the Viennese working class, those desperate heroes who died out of moral stubbornness, and whom the Red salons were calling "Social Fascists" at the very moment they were falling under the cannonades of Fascism.

During these years, besides his own poetry, Spender was working on the series of translations of Rainer Maria Rilke which he published with J.B.Leishman. These translations have had a tremendous effect on contemporary British verse, greater possibly than Spender's own poetry, and, I believe, mostly for the bad. Rilke is extremely popular with young writers in England, but even for those who read German, and few do, he seems to come to them as he has been transformed by Spender. Now Rilke may have lived in a cloud of patchouli, but it was a well defined cloud. If Stefan George may be said to have written German as though it was English, Rilke certainly wrote it with the clarity of French. There are few modern poets with a more active vocabulary. His nouns and adjectives are sharp and precise and present immediate images, his verbs positively writhe with

einfühlung. There is none of this in the Spender-Leishman translations. Everything is reduced to an amorphous, ruminative melancholy,
thought about thought, words about words. All is imprecision, mood,
like formless background music played by a good orchestra, Werner
Jansen's sobbing violins accompanying the trivial pathos of a point-
less movie.

Young writers were turning away from the objectivism of Grigson
and his school, because it was an objectivism without content, the
photograph of a meal instead of a good dinner. Empson's verbal
puzzles grew quickly boring, Auden's Byronic glitter had turned to
brass, the Spender-Leishman Rilke gave the prestige of a great name
to a vague, hypnotic sentimentality. The end of its influence is not
yet. At the present time, the most conspicuous, though not the most
important, difference between American and British verse is the rhetorical imprecision and verbal lassitude of the latter.

Spender's own verse may suffer from similar faults at times, but it
contains no cheap-jack solutions, no political or religious confidence
games, no smart aleck stylistic trickery. He never made any bold
public statements about it, but he quietly moved away from those
who suffered most from such faults. Reading him, one has the sense
of a man trying desperately hard to be absolutely honest. I think it
is for this reason that he is still a living influence on younger writers
in England.

In *The Oxford Book of Modern Verse*, Yeats had noticed another break
with the dominant style of the time, and had prophesied that here
was very likely a forerunner of a future literary revolution. I refer
of course to George Barker. If the work of the previous generation
was rhetorical, if the self was hidden behind panaceas for the world
ill, in Barker, rhetoric is pushed to the critical point where it turns
into its opposite. The world ill is taken into the self. Barker seems
to swallow the sick public soul, neutralize it with his own spiritual
intoxications, and then cast it forth, and his own occult inwardness
along with it. This may not be the most lucid description of what
is actually an impressive and exciting artistic process to observe, but
it is obviously far removed from the ambulatory, jaded eye of Louis

MacNeice. Barker's verse is not just exhortative, like a political speech, it really is excited, its dynamism does not come from a rhetorical formula, but from a disturbed and disturbing internal vortex. Barker has often been compared to Blake. He is rather like Blake, but like Blake in reverse, a mirror image. Blake objectified his internal conflicts, not the absurd "conflicts" of the Freudian clinic but the actual struggle that always goes on in the awakened soul of man. He made mythological dramatis personae out of the elements of the self, and set them at war with each other. In many ways his method was not unlike that later developed by Carl Jung. Barker, on the other hand, has taken the figures of the collective unconscious which have assumed a terrible reality in our time, shorn them of their hypostatization, and set them at war within his own self. If this were the end of the matter, the situation would be uncontrollable, and unendurable, and would soon degenerate into madness or total irresponsibility. Barker's earliest work did, often, seem to stop here, but in later work the savior, the harrier of this interior hell, becomes more and more manifest. He is, as one might guess, the Divine Eros fleshed, the simple abandon and finding of the self in the act of love. In style too, Barker resembles a reversed Blake. Where Blake hunted for the particulars, the inescapable objectivity to garb his subjective vision, Barker pushes the subjective hallucination to the point where it takes body for others. This is what some Surrealists say, programmatically, that they attempt. Barker does not try to reach a predetermined goal in the reader's consciousness by the use of psychiatric devices. He is, with great passion, a kind of person.

If Auden dominated the recent past, Dylan Thomas dominates the present. There can be no question but that he is the most influential young poet writing in England today. The unanimity with which everyone except unreconstructed Stalinists and tame magazine versifiers points to him as the greatest phenomenon in contemporary poetry is simply astonishing. Considering that something like this was once the case with Auden, it bodes ill for Thomas' reputation some ten years hence. However, it was not always thus. When he first appeared, he was greeted with tolerant but embarrassed consternation, as though he had just made a muss. Spender said his poems dripped like water out of a tap. Symons said he twisted words to the shape of his reader's ears. He reminded Hugh Gordon Porteus of an unconducted tour of Bedlam, or a night out in a land of gibbering highbrows. And so on down the line, it was as though something had escaped that had been locked up in Wild Wales since the Synod of Whitby, and was clanking its chains and yammering in the Rectory drawing room. Something terribly unbritish seemed to be happening. It was.

Thomas is far more shameless than Barker. He doesn't wear his heart on his sleeve. He takes you by the neck and rubs your nose in it. He hits you across the face with a reeking, bloody heart, a heart full of worms and needles and black blood and thorns, a werewolf heart. This is the hairy wenid that has been peeping through the shutters since the Saxon drew his lines in Shropshire. In the old age of the English, it has burst in the door and settled down on top of the Sunday dinner. At first the noise was deafening, adders, she-bears, witches on the mountain, exploding pit-heads, menstruating babies, hounds with red ears, Welsh revivalists throwing dynamite and semen in all directions. Thomas smote the Philistine as hard a blow with one small book, *Eighteen Poems*, as Swinburne had with *Poems and Ballads*.

The terrific racket has long since died down. It is possible now to inspect the early Thomas coolly and discover what he is saying and what he is talking about. Many elements went to form his idiom, all bound together by the reeling excitement of a poetry-intoxicated schoolboy. First, I would say, Hopkins' metric and his peculiar, neurasthenic irritability of perception; second, Hart Crane, whom Thomas greatly resembles; third, possibly, translations of Rimbaud and *Maldoror*, though he could have got most of this from Crane; fourth, Welsh poetry and mythology, with its gnarled metrics and its imagery of a barbaric and forested country, a land literally wild; fifth, the Old Testament, as it came to him through the savage Welsh Nonconformity; sixth, a mass of uncontrolled, boyish omnivorous reading: detective stories, translated Surrealism, "science fiction," horror tales, sex books, occultism, Shakespeare, Blake, Lawrence, Henry Miller, A.E.Waite, Arthur Machen, an orgy of literary sensationalism. Yeats once said of somebody that he remained a barbarian because he was born in the provinces and never had a chance to associate with a man of real culture until he was grown. Thomas wrote as though he had never met a human being who had ever bathed or used a toothbrush. On the other hand, there is nothing squalid about it. Thomas wrote like a savage chief on a scalp-taking expedition amongst the palefaces. He definitely belonged to the heroes of Toynbee's "external proletariat" not to the drudges and tramps of his "internal proletariat."

The early Thomas does not add up to just another barbaric yawp, however heroic. It all meant something. Possibly it was a raucous and primitive cry, but it was the most primitive and terrible cry in the world, the cry of parturition, the dual cry of mother and child. If Jung served to elucidate Barker somewhat, Rank can serve even better for Thomas. Most of his early poetry is about the agony and horror of being born and of childbirth. The substance of Rank's *The Artist* is that the artist is, psychologically, his own mother. Few have ever realized this as thoroughly and as violently as Thomas. For him the crucifixion and the virgin birth are one simultaneous process, archetypes of the act, or rather catastrophe, of the creative consciousness. Other men, Baudelaire for instance, have talked about their agonies as creators. Thomas discovered poetry on his hands like blood, and screamed aloud.

I mentioned that Thomas resembled Hart Crane. This is as far as Crane was able to go — the horror of creative birth. I once heard a preacher say that Christ's agony in the garden and his relations with his mother showed the terrible responsibility of sonship. Certainly this phrase can be applied to the early Thomas and to Crane. Crane's solution, his myth, the Bridge, did not work. It is possible to worship the mother, the father, the self, but a saving symbol cannot be made of the umbilicus alone, it must be connected to something. So Crane's poetry and his personality began to break up and deteriorate. This has not happened to Thomas. His recent work has developed in the only way that it could from such antecedents, towards a deeper mystical insight. He has moved away from the old, excited, tempestuous possession, and toward the humility and calm of ecstatic vision. So his influences have been, in his later poems, those entranced Welshmen, Vaughan and Herbert.

I do not believe that Thomas is in any danger of falling into the appliqué metaphysical verse once fashionable in the Empson circle and in America. If an atheist don tries to write like Donne or Crashaw, the result is pretty sorry stuff. If one actually has an intensely religious, baroque personality, one doesn't have to try, one falls naturally into step with one's ancestors. I think it quite possible that the religious expression of the baroque sensibility is not the most profound of the varieties of religious experience, but it is certainly genuine, and it is certainly Thomas' vision, thoroughly and sincerely. The deepest regions of the soul may have been accessible only to the sculptors of the Bon Dieu of Amiens, and the Yakshini of the gate of Sanchi, or to the Zen landscapists, but it would be wicked to quarrel with the explorations of an El Greco or a Grunewald when they are undertaken once again in a naughty world.

Thomas' impact was not just literary, it was in a special sense social, a cultural coup d'état. Nothing less like a Marxist from a Good School being raffish at a country house could be imagined. After Thomas, literature was wide open to others than the sons of gentlemen, if they could find some way to keep alive. This is far more important than it might seem in America. And it is surprising how many of the significant younger poets in Britain today did not go to a Public School or to "either" University. In this regard too, Thomas resembled Hart Crane. He had the same sort of pariah integrity, and made the same violent assault upon official culture. The thin erudition of the previous generation, the result of judicious schooling and back numbers of *The Criterion*, seemed idle stuff beside his wolfing of books. I think it important too that in Thomas the spiritual underworld of a suppressed civilization, the Celtic shadow cast by the Saxon torch, found voice and took flesh. Even today, however much he has quieted down, one still feels that a different culture speaks through him. This accounts for his barbaric aristocracy. The Highland "kings" encountered by Sam Johnson may have been barefoot, illiterate and lousy, but they were far more aristocratic than the Whig lords in their vast houses to the South, and more regal than the German bourgeois on his throne of compromise.

About this time, the poetry of W.R.Rodgers began to appear in magazines. Although it is easy to write extensively about Barker and Thomas and still say something important, it is not so easy to do with Rodgers, and that is just the point. There is nothing spectacular about him. In fact his verse has a sort of dogged earnestness about it, although it is far from pedestrian. His great virtue is that he speaks for himself. He is relatively free of the fashionable influences of the day, and he has almost no visible connection with the previous generation. His work is as simple and profound as he can make it. His effects are achieved quietly, and they are always the direct outcome of integral experience. He never depends upon secondary references to chic reading matter and current postures. One of his peculiar virtues is a special sonority — a sort of gong and woodwind depth and color of long vowel and labial, sibilant, and nasal music which is, as it were, a kind of counter Hopkins. Hopkins' baroque irritability expressed itself in staccato vowels and plosives and stops and a restive metrical distortion. Rodgers has the confidence of Solesmes or the pre-Bach organists — the marching, sure, unperturbed musical development of Byrd and Gibbons and Frescobaldi — a Protestant, or at least pre-Tridentine answer to Hopkins. The quality I associate most clearly with his work is a rugged, protestant magnanimity, courteous and polished enough superficially, but with, still underneath, a certain strongly masculine gaucherie. The comparison that springs to mind is Andrew Marvel. All one has to do is list these qualities to see how unusual and refreshing they would seem in the literary atmosphere of the time of his first appearance. It is difficult to measure Rodgers' influence, because, to the best of my knowledge, it has been effortless, he has never made any attempt to wield any. I think, however, that it has been considerable; depth, expression, simplicity, and integrity are certainly marked qualities in the work of many who have come after him.

There was nothing programmatic about the new direction taken by Barker, Thomas and Rodgers. They were simply different from the generation that preceded them. Very soon, however, their innovations, especially Thomas', were reduced to a program. The New Apocalypse was a well organized movement of the continental type, almost as well organized as the Auden circle or Breton's Surrealism. At one time it included George Fraser, Norman McCaig, Vernon Watkins, J. F. Hendry, and Henry Treece. Today only Treece and Hendry still seem to think of themselves as Apocalyptics.

In the beginning there was a slight air of reformed Marxist self-consciousness about Apocalypse. Lip service at least was still paid to the long since foundered Revolution. Sometimes there was almost a suspicion that the Apocalyptics looked forward to a day when there would be an Apocalyptic majority in the House of Commons with the Book of Revelations as a party platform. Certainly there was an effort to colonize the areas in the consciousness opened up by Thomas in the name of the main tradition of the revolt of the previous period, and at the same time to personalize the Revolution.

As one looks back on Apocalypse, it is apparent that the name was fortunately chosen. Not only did it fit the times, but it meant more than its proponents realized. It conjured up memories of D. H. Lawrence and Albert Schweitzer. It implied what the latter called an "eschatological world view," a morality based on the assumption that we live in the imminence of judgment and destruction by fire, which happened to be literally true in a moderate degree.

To quote from the Apocalyptic program: "1) That human, including poetic, development must be towards wholeness, and must recognize heart no less than head, the dream, no less than the waking world. 2) That man has become the victim of mechanization, and must be freed if his personality is to survive; which freedom may come via Myth, Imagination (in Coleridge's sense) or a personal Religion as opposed to a Mass Creed." This sounds not unlike Jolas' valiant and vain effort to shift the base of Surrealism from Freud to Jung. Like Jolas, the Apocalypse failed as a movement, the participants scattered, aesthetically speaking, and some of them seem, today, a little ashamed of their connection.

I believe Apocalypse failed because it was not a radical enough break with the past. It still bore marks of both literary Marxism and Surrealism. You cannot personalize a revolution which is, by definition, as impersonal as an earthquake. The science of seismology has no place for human values. The problem must be approached from the other end. One must revolutionize the concept and position of personality, so degraded by our dying civilization. This is not just a rhetorical antithesis. In fact, it is what happened. Today Treece is one of the editors of the yearbook *Transformation*. As I see it, *Transformation* is attempting to do something similar to what Eliot did with *The Criterion*. It is trying to give England a new ideological center, this time a "Personalist" one, around which can be gathered a new generation, and from which all aspects of our culture could be approached consistently, judged and revalued. It is significant that *Transformation* has come more and more under the influence of the recently deceased Russian Orthodox philosopher and theologian Berdyaev. At the same time, Berdyaev himself had been reforming his philosophy into what can only be called a new and dynamic variety of religious anarchism.

Treece himself has often been called an imitator of Thomas. It is true that Treece wrote an enthusiastic brochure about him when Thomas' total oeuvre was exactly *Eighteen Poems*, but there really is not a great deal of resemblance. Both are Welsh, but Thomas speaks, as I said, for the aristocratic underworld of a suppressed civilization. He is always the Druid, passing on his occult wisdom within the sound of the church bells. Treece uses a material much closer to folk art, to the changeless, gnomic tales of the universal peasant, Teuton, Celt or Finn. In fact, his best poems are very Germanic, märchen poetry, Grimm capsules. In spite of his Personalist professions, it is very difficult to come at the personal core in his poems, they slip away into anonymity, like handicrafts or Gothic woodcarvings.

Originally greatly under the influence of D. H. Lawrence, D. S. Savage has developed along similar lines. He makes the rather acute point that a thoroughly integrated person would not go about calling himself a "personalist," but his book, *The Personal Principle* is a review of the masters of a generation, Lawrence, Yeats, Eliot, Crane, Auden, in terms of their ability to achieve personal integration or integral personality. The fact that he gives critical approval only to Harold

Monro casts a certain suspicion on his method, but the book has some penetrating insights and has been very influential. His poetry certainly shows forth an integral personality lost in the violent, noisy, squalid darkness of a de-personalized and collapsing society. Savage, once the British editor of the forthrightly Lawrentian magazine *Phoenix*, is one of the possible channels through which D. H. Lawrence has re-emerged as a powerful, even dominant influence. However, I think this was more a spontaneous and diffuse matter. After all, his books are still accessible. Of the major figures of the period immediately after the first war, he is, with Herbert Read, the only one who could be said to be potent today. It is not just the superficial aspects of Lawrence, his abstract merits as a novelist or poet which are taken seriously, but his philosophy of life and his aesthetics. *Fantasia of the Unconscious*, *Apocalypse*, the posthumous papers and letters, certain of the more didactic poems, are being read by younger men, not just because they enjoy them, but because, largely, they agree with them.

Another major influence which is difficult to measure is that of Henry Miller. All over the world Miller has acted as the liberator of a generation. Not since Ibsen has an author had so catalytic an effect, nor has the reaction produced by his catalysis been so violent. Miller is not as great an artist as Lawrence or Ibsen or Neitzche or Strindberg, other, similar prophets of modern man, but his voice has been especially loud and clear because he spoke when everyone else kept silent. No other person of his generation has had so great an influence on the young who were being asked to die for very dubious reasons in a second world war. I think it should be realized that those of combat age believed very little of what they were told by those who were not. Miller expressed their disbelief, and their emergent beliefs, not just their distrust of the putative aims of their governments, but their rejection of the whole social lie of a diseased and tawdry civilization, and their hope to find a new foundation for life in a cleansed and redeemed love relationship. There were other things to be found in Miller, too — his apocalyptic style, his disdain of fancy writing and all the donnish recipes for ambiguity and chic, and, most important, his rejection of the State and all other complexes of power and irresponsibility as evil hoaxes. In the years when a monstrous social fraud was destroying the world, Miller pointed out that the Emperor did not have any clothes on.

There is another side of Miller, his quietism, his ability to bend in the storm, his shunning of the violence of urban culture and literary conflict, his simple appetites and good nature, all of which add up to a kind of sensual Taoism or spiritualized hedonism. It is this aspect of Miller which is most pronounced in the work of his friend Lawrence Durrell. In the days when Miller's *Tropics* were creating a sensation, Durrell produced a somewhat similar novel, *The Black Book*. As a study of moral exhaustion it has seldom been equaled. There is a certain naïveté about Miller, he is very much like the Eighteenth Century naïve writer Restif de la Bretonne, but there is nothing naïve about *The Black Book*. It is as though Pascal had turned his scientific and passionate eye on the behavior of some trivial diabolist of the gutter. Having produced so accurate a diagnosis of the world ill, Durrell retired to the island of Corfu. There, eventually, the war caught up with him, but not until he had perfected a poetic expression of uniquely self sufficient tranquillity. Since then he seems to have undergone many of the vicissitudes of a moderately successful diplomatic career, but the interior idyll which he constructed for himself has remained undisturbed, certainly an indication of its authenticity.

Miller was not quite alone. In England at least, one other older man spoke out, clearly and forcefully, Herbert Read. Sometimes I think Read is a little like Dryden. His personal development has had an unfortunate coincidence with historical movements and changes in the popular mind. He has been any number of things, or at least he has been influenced by a large number of popular intellectual vagaries — Thomism, Humanism, Marxism, Freudianism, Surrealism, and so on. I believe this has not been because he was a bandwagon rider, for he has always climbed off the bandwagon before the calliope struck up a march, but because he has been very much alive, and awake to, and accessible to, the storms that have swept over Twentieth Century thought. Then too, there are a number of attitudes, principles and tastes which he has stuck to and never changed. He has always been a Platonist of a somewhat heretical sort. He has always been interested in psychoanalysis, not just in Freud, but in all aspects of the subject, and seems to have read extensively all the masters. He has always had a strong sense of caste, of being a Platonic "guardian," somehow, by virtue of his sensibility and insight, like Confucius' gentleman, chun tzu, responsible for the public health. He has always been genuinely humane, always searching for an organic life in an organic society. He has always been interested in education, especially an education that would develop, as primitive society does, the intuitive, feeling, aesthetic, aspects of the personality, as well as the reasoning and manipulative. Lastly, he has always had a special attachment to Wordsworth, in whom he has found, down the years, not Marxism, Humanism, Freudianism, Surrealism, and so on, but what he, Herbert Read, meant by those things.

When the second war came, Read stuck to the position he had assumed after the first one, he remained a pacifist. He had come out of the Spanish War years, the years of the Moscow Trials, convinced of the soundness and necessity of anarchism. He says somewhere that anarchism possibly may sound impractical, but certainly less impractical than the modern capitalist nation-state would sound if described to someone in another civilization; and it is obvious that nothing else will work; any form of State is bound to fail from now on, and fail disastrously.

Further, in various critical writings, Read had built up a whole philosophy of what he called Romanticism. It was an odd Romanticism, which always included the permanent elements of his mind I mentioned above. Its poetics was based on Plato, Milton's phrase, "simple, sensuous and passionate," the *Preface to Lyrical Ballads*, and Rilke's *Letter to a Young Poet*. It seems to me that this is a Romanticism which would fitly describe most Greek and Roman poetry; and since, in addition, he has distinguished himself, the Romantic, from T. S. Eliot, the Classicist, I must confess that I for one, am all at sea. But no matter.

In Read it is possible to see all the strains of the time converge. His recent writing on art approximates the position of the Catholic anarchist Eric Gill. He speaks of the necessity for an organic art, deeply imbedded in life and growing from it, and not hung on the walls of museums. It happens that as Lawrence lay dying in Vence he was writing a review of Gill's first book. Lawrence and Read share with Gill a whole world view, not just an aesthetic — the rejection of mechanistic civilization, sterile scientism, and topheavy rationalism, the quest for a true integrality of the person, a belief in the importance of sacramental marriage. This is also Berdyaev's philosophy, and with him too, and with all the others, Read shares a belief in the importance of ritual, reverence for life, the reverent performance of the acts of life, sacramentalism. Now "reverence for life" is a key term in the philosophy of Albert Schweitzer, and Schweitzer is the father of the "apocalyptic world view." Similarly, Read has spoken of the essential characteristic of a humane society, a reverence for other persons — that one should treat his fellow not as a he, she, or it, but as a thou, in the words of Martin Buber. So all the threads draw together. It is well that they should be drawn together in Read. He is incomparably the most civilized as he is the eldest of the poets of the Romantic movement, and he is probably the only one who has read all the testaments of what, by now it should be obvious, is not just a new school of poetry, but a new world outlook — from Chuang Tzu to Henry Miller and from Carl Jung to Martin Buber. Also, and not least important, he is a highly polished artist, and the effect of his wartime collection of verse, *A World Within A War*, owed much to the sheer perfection of its writing. It said the same things the younger men were saying, but it said them with a maturity, depth and finesse of which most of them were, at least as yet, incapable.

Read was not alone in advocating anarchism. During the Spanish War the anarchist paper *Spain and the Revolution*, formerly, and now again, *Freedom*, was one of the most reliable sources of information for British radicals. Most of the other radical papers were at least tendentious, and in the case of the Stalinists simply mendacious. Then too, the impression made by the Catalan anarchists on the British volunteers and observers was, in a personal sense, revolutionary. Their bravura, and the genuine freedom of their lives, were poles removed from the dry, doctrinaire, circumspect, sociological behavior of the traditional British Left. British radicalism, no matter how red, was bound up in the strait-jacket of Fabianism and Methodism, and when it, or rather its younger representatives under arms, encountered hot nights, bad cognac, dark eyes, sweat and dynamite, the strait-jacket exploded. In many ways, British anarchism is a revolt in favor of all those beautiful things in life which aren't British. Spain introduced another note, via Garcia Lorca in literature, "Black Spain," with its Muslim fascination with death and sweating lust and danger and pain, unbritish subjects hitherto ignored by the best taste. The young anarchist poet George Woodcock started a magazine *Now*, at first a most unpretentious poetry sheet, and later a quite influential paper. Originally purely literary, it gradually came to encompass most of the aspects of the new tendency and its catholicity of editorial policy was probably a shock to those who expect of a radical publication the heresy hunting and dogmatism of the Marxist journals. Similarly, Woodcock's own poetry has been anything but tendentious.

With the exception of Read, Alex Comfort is the nearest thing to a systematic Romantic. He has a well thought out and consistent philosophy of life with which he seems to be able to encounter most contingencies, and by which his literary practice is illuminated and reinforced. Central to it is the concept of the personality at war with death—physical death, or the mechanization of the State, and all the other institutions of irresponsibility and spiritual sloth. With Comfort, physician and experimental physiologist, the arts of literature and medicine may reinforce each other. Certainly he has a maturity and grasp, a sense of mastery of his material, which is rare in so young a man. He has a universality about him in many ways reminiscent of Albert Schweitzer. I would be inclined to say that he, Woodcock, and Savage are the most remarkable of the young men who came first to prominence during the War, and it is significant that they are all anarchists, "personalists," and pacifists. In his critical book, *What I Mean by Apocalypse* Treece also calls himself an anarchist.

I say young men, because the war years also produced a number of remarkable women poets. It seems somewhat false to discuss a writer on the basis of her sex, as a woman poet, or worse, poetess. Still, poets like Anne Ridler, Kathleen Raine, Lynette Roberts, Brenda Chamberlain, Eithne Wilkins, Denise Levertov, Alison Boodson, all share an intense femininity, if nothing else. The previous period was not very strong on women poets, I can think of none offhand. It is not just that the men were off to war and the field was left open which brought out so many women, but rather, I think, the reorientation towards personal expression, and away from construction and political rhetoric. So these women have written about the things that matter, not about current delusions — lovers and husbands leaving for war, babies, death, birth, love, all subjects frowned on in earlier years. Certainly if Auden and his friends ever had any babies, they never wrote about them.

Nicholas Moore, although he has figured prominently in the growth of the Romantic movement, both as an editor and as the personal friend of many of its leading figures, stands somewhat outside the general picture. It seems to me that he owes more to American poetry, especially to Wallace Stevens and to the Fugitives group. He is past master of a relaxed, civilized, conversational tone. It is really amazing how natural his lines sound. It is so casual and offhand until one pays close attention to what he is talking about, and then it turns out that he is one of the most intense and visionary of the Romantics, and a consummate craftsman of effects of great subtlety. It is as though Baudelaire were to be rewritten, over the biscuits and sherry, by Walter Bagehot. I might point out that this idiosyncratic mode of expression has no similarity to the "public speech" of the previous period.

Fred Murnau, a Czech emigré living in England, has been very influential, as an editor, a poet, and personally, in the development of the new Romanticism. His work, written in German and translated by Ernest Sigler, has reinforced the tendencies which first appeared in the Spender-Leishman Rilke. His poetry has a dreamy, nostalgic sorrow about it, reminiscent of autumn evenings in the Wienerwald before the other war, lights on the river at Budapest, Smetana's *Moldau*, Brahms at his most ruminative. It isn't about any of these things, but it is certainly saturated in the special sentiment of bygone Middle Europe. In poets like Denise Levertov this tendency reaches its height in slow, pulsating rhythms, romantic melancholy and undefined nostalgia. Once these qualities would have been considered blemishes, today they are outstanding virtues. For the first time, schwarmerei enters English verse.

Has the Romantic Movement reached its apogee, produced an idiom, an expression which will be as definitive as the best work of Auden was for his period? The idiom, yes. There can be no question but that a new and different medium has been developed, but it is doubtful if the major works in that idiom have been written. I do not believe that Thomas should be grouped with the Romantics, anymore than Donne should be grouped with Shelley. Spender, Barker and Rodgers are really precursors of the movement rather than members. The younger people are still developing, some of them so fast it has been hard to keep up with them.

The religious personalism and political anarchism which provide the dominant ideology of the movement is still young as a Weltanschauung. It is not something taken over from their bureaucratic betters by poetic fellow travellers, but has been developed, in situ and from the heart by Read, Comfort, Woodcock, Savage, Treece, and the rest, as they went along. So it can still stand an enormous amount of critical shaping. Its relations with the orthodox "anarchist movement," a rather doctrinaire body at the best, as well as its relations with Catholic and Protestant Christianity, are still to be defined. At least it can be said that contemporary English thought has avoided the diffuse, eclectic, heterodox religiosity represented by Huxley, Heard, Isherwood and other Anglo-Hollywood mystics, and, on the other hand, has shown no signs of being captivated by the masochistic kitsch which passes for profundity amongst the continental Existentialists and certain circles in New York. That is an undeniable blessing.

There is one place where many of the leading ideas of the New Romanticism are not new, in fact they are part of the accepted consensus of informed opinion, and that is the Catholic Church. Contemporary Catholic apologetic has made much of the importance of the person, the value of ritual and sacramentalism as an expression of respect for life, the drive of the modern State towards mechanical evil, the significance of marriage as a channel of spiritual realization, the irresponsibility of modern warfare. So it is that there has been a certain convergence. The wave of revolt against modern materialism has brought some poets into the Church, other Catholic poets have been fairly closely identified with Romanticism from its inception, and Catholic anarchists and personalists like Gill and Berdyaev have had a great influence in England.

Kathleen Raine, Anne Ridler, Norman Nicholson, all Catholics, are amongst the best poets writing in England today. Kathleen Raine's work is remarkable for her concentration on absolute purity of sensibility. She reminds me of the modern French Catholic verse which has learned from Valéry. Originally the youngest member of the Cambridge group, her work has always seemed far more intense and ethereal than theirs. In recent years personal tragedy and conversion to the Church have given it new poignancy and meaning. She is not the least member of a tradition which includes Christina Rossetti, Alice Meynell, and Michael Field. Anne Ridler writes about love, marriage, children, the loneliness of parting, all the simple, sacramental facts of a woman's life, a sort of Tertiary Franciscan poetry. Some of her later work, possibly influenced by Eliot's *Four Quartets*, has moved on to larger mystical and moral themes. Nicholson is a strange exception to the general run of English poetry today. He lives in one of the most beautiful of English counties, Cumberland, withdrawn from the distractions, the tragedies and vast issues and petty spites of life in the capital, and his verse is withdrawn too. It has the same peace, care, and mystical stillness that Wordsworth sought, and sometimes found, in the same region. There are others who seem to be on the border of Catholicism. Nigel Heseltine and Rayner Heppenstall (two of the most easily confused names in contemporary letters!) both write an ambiguous, Gnostic sort of poetry, which, however heterodox, certainly makes very free use of Catholic symbolism. Derek Savage, again, has much in common with contemporary Catholic radicalism, and David Gascoyne's *Gravel Pit Field*, whatever its sectarian religious background, if any, is one of the finest mystical poems I know.

Thomas, Treece, Watkins, Lynette Roberts, Keidrych Rhys, Brenda Chamberlain, Heseltine, Glyn Jones, Woodcock, are all Welsh. There

XXXI

is a more or less deliberate Welsh School which centers around Rhys' magazine *Wales*. A heavy odor of the modernism of the Twenties still hangs over the poetry in *Wales*. Most of this stuff is dreadful and I have not included it. Keidrych Rhys and Lynette Roberts, both fine poets, are, however, somewhat blemished by it. Brenda Chamberlain is, I feel, one of the very few (another is Eithne Wilkins) younger poets who has been able to recapture and transmit or transmute some of the technical, syntactical, psychological devices and felicities of those days into the Romantic idiom. She is one of the poets in Britain whose work I think may, by a thesis–antithesis–synthesis development in relation to the previous generation, presage the growth of a new, post-romantic style. Although there is considerable talk of a Welsh renascence, most of the poetry of Welsh writers has entered immediately into the main stream of British verse. I think it is significant however, that London has not produced anything resembling its proportion of writers. This seems to be true always of decaying capitals; generation by generation, the major Roman poets come from farther and farther away from Rome.

Contemporary Scots writing, on the other hand, has nothing to do with England. The Scots Renascence is dominated by Hugh Macdiarmid. Someone once said of him that he had done for Scots verse what Parnell did for Irish politics, a doubtful, though fitting compliment. It is certainly true that the Renascence is so under his influence that it suffers from his faults and is limited by his crotchets. He has plenty of both and to spare. In fact, he is regarded, South of the Border, as pretty much of a professional oddy. This is probably true, but it is unjust. He is unquestionably one of the most important writers in the British Isles, and a genuine world literary figure, but he is also a deliberate eccentric, a man of very mixed and incongruous notions, all held with the maximum bigotry. He seems to be a Bolshevik, a Scotch Republican, and sometimes talks as though he were a Stuart Legitimist as well. Recently, noticing the commotion to the South, he has added that he is an anarchist, Stalinism being only a technique for achieving anarchism! His reading is immense, not just omnivorous, but gluttonous, and it is served up in large chunks of ill-digested quotation at the most opportune and inopportune times in everything he writes, prose or verse. In many ways he resembles

Ezra Pound, and at one time they had considerable admiration for each other. His dislike of Auden and his circle is extreme, and dates back to the very beginning. Possibly this is due to the fact that he is, like Laura Riding, one of Auden's most carefully concealed "ancestors." All the Auden program is there, "public speech"(?), Marxism, rationalism (he has actually said that Stalinism should be called "mentalism" because it is the doctrine that man can save himself by the exercise of his reason; however, he has said other things, completely contradictory) sentimentalism, the attack on the Public School and Suburbia and the Empire Mind, and the constant portrayal of the signs of death in bourgeois society. In my opinion it is all done much better, as it was done much earlier, by Macdiarmid. A common criticism of Macdiarmid is that he does not write a true, dialectical Scotch, but a dictionary language — made up by consulting a Scots dictionary and substituting Doric wherever possible for English. This produces an inorganic and unnatural lingo never spoken by man, something like babu English, and motivated really by a factitious pseudo-nationalism. This is a difficult criticism to assess. It depends largely on whether Macdiarmid gets away with it — sometimes he does not — but very often he does, brilliantly. Possibly the Scots words in poems like *The Watergaw*, *The Eemis-stane*, *O wha's been here afore me, lass*, come from different dialects — but the effect is integral. Possibly the synthetic character of the vocabulary is what gives some of the earlier longer poems the sound of jargon. The later long elegies seem more compact and natural, as far as the use of Scots goes. At the present time Macdiarmid is writing long poems, full of quotations from many languages, and jam-packed with every notion, important or not, contradictory or not, that crosses his mind. These things are fun to read, but I can think of no principle on which one could select any passage for anthologizing. His early lyrics are amongst the finest in the Scots language, some of them the equal of Burns. By contemporary taste they have one grave fault. Although they have an unforgettable music and an atmosphere as weird as it is poignant, they are strangely impersonal. Even more than Pound, behind lyric or elegy it is very hard to find a living man.

This could hardly be said of the Gaelic poet Sorley Maclean. His poems have been compared to the songs of the *Tain bo Cualgne*, the Cuchulain epic, and to Simonides, but there is no doubt that they are about himself. If other people can write poetry like this in Gaelic, there is no question but what it will again be a living language. Although he has been translated by others into Scots verse, notably by Douglas Young, I prefer his own prose-poem translations which are at least as remarkable as the somewhat similar work of Lady Gregory.

William Soutar's verse is unique. Paralyzed for many years, he lay in bed, looked out through an immense window into his garden, and wrote innumerable poems - thousands - both in English and Scots. Most of them are pure and honest, but really occasional verse. A few are startling things to come on in modern literature. They have a directness and absolute simplicity, and at the same time a sweetness and perfection that has very seldom been equalled. These are poems that at their best rise to near levels occupied only by Cowper. Soutar, incidently, was, though bedridden, a very active pacifist and opponent of the State.

I have included a section from J. B. Macleod's *Ecliptic*, a poem published a good while ago, but in my opinion undeservedly forgotten. Pushed aside by the highly organized claque of the Thirties, Macleod seems to have given up poetry, which is a great pity. Ruthven Todd and George Fraser, though both Scottish, seem in recent years to have been pretty much absorbed into English literature. It happens that both write verse characterized by directness and honesty and unabashed sentiment — not unlike the prose of F. Scott Fitzgerald. I should not be surprised if this special medium which they share should not become more common in the near future.

I have not printed anyone simply because he was a "soldier poet" or was killed in the war, anymore than I have included anyone because he was a conscientious objector, a cripple or a woman. I do not believe that such things have much to do with poetry. On the other hand, I agree with Yeats that, by and large, war poetry is pretty dreadful stuff. It serves its purpose in its day, but whatever the pity of its circumstance, it is soon forgotten. Owen, Yeats to the contrary, is remembered, but he would have been, whatever he wrote about. The second war had its Owens, grave losses to British letters, but most of them too young to estimate exactly what they would have grown into. One man's death, however, was an unquestionable literary catastrophe. Keith Douglas from his very first poems as an Oxford undergraduate, had a control of his medium which only is given to those who are going to become very great writers. I consider his poems beyond question the best written under combat in the second war. Not only that, but far more than Todd or Fraser, I think he pointed a new direction towards simplicity and candor, which is very possibly going to be the dominant mode of the next phase of British poetry.

There are several poets whom I have not been able to fit into this survey. Some lie outside the general pattern, like Sean Jennett, Eithne Wilkins, Vernon Watkins, Terence Tiller, Laurie Lee. Others, like Allott, Spencer, Madge, belong in style if not in age to the preceding period. I have, as I said, tried to include everyone, of whatever style, whom I consider a good poet, who was born in 1908 or later. Besides the Scots, I have made only two exceptions that I know of; one is Vernon Watkins, who only began to appear with the Apocalypse, who is allied to, if not part of, the Romantic movement; and the other, Charles Wrey Gardiner, whose serious poetic development dates only from his meeting with Comfort, Moore, Murnau and the rest. His journal of one year of Romanticism, family, money and erotic difficulties, buzz bombs and passionate conversation in intellectual pubs, *The Dark Thorn,* is the best picture of the world of contemporary British poetry which I know.

In closing I might mention the more important periodicals. Magazines of the previous period, like *Scrutiny, New Verse, New Signatures, Twentieth Century Verse,* have all perished, and with them, many of those of the Romantic movement, such as *Seven* and *Kingdom Come.* Strictly within the field of poetry the magazine that has moved the most mountains has been Tambimuttu's (the name is Singhalese) *Poetry London.* In the first issue, on the very eve of war, Tambi published a "Letter" which sounded less like a literary manifesto than a series of excerpts from the Tao Te Ching and Chuang Tzu. Speaking as an Oriental, with perfect confidence in his non-European background, he was able to marshall a "history" of Western civilization in terms of causes, diagnosis, pathology remedies, behavior and prognosis, with a cogency and insight which very few English poets could have mustered. The effect seems to have been galvanic. Poets rallied to him immediately. For all the years of the war he published the best verse and the newest verse in England. Recently PL has come out only sporadically, at long intervals. Without Tambimuttu the picture might have been different, more like America where the generation that came up during the war is still struggling for a hearing.

Somewhat later Wrey Gardiner began to open the pages of *Poetry Quarterly*, originally a pretty dull, conventional, Poetry Club sort of magazine, to the new movement. Soon he was in the midst of the stream. *Poetry Quarterly* has been less erratically published than *Poetry London*; once convinced, Gardiner has persevered with greater concentration and singleness of purpose than Tambimuttu. His publishing house, Grey Walls Press, also issues a yearbook, *New Road*, edited by Fred Murnau or Alex Comfort, or both together, which has provided a more permanent medium of publication for the Romantic movement, and which also prints plays, fiction and criticism.

Both Grey Walls and *Poetry London* also publish books of verse. Routledge, a large, old and well-established firm, of which Herbert Read is an editor, has published small booklets of many of the Romantic poets, and it has published them early, while they were still young, and at very modest prices. We do things differently in America, where Wallace Stevens and William Carlos Williams are still known to reviewers as "young poets of the experimental generation."

John Lehmann's yearbook, *New Writing*, well known in America, has not shown much sympathy with Romanticism. Lehmann has tended to concentrate on his own circle of poets, most of whom I find very uninteresting, or to publish well recognized names. Terence Tiller and Laurie Lee, both very fine, somewhat "classical" poets, the latter much influenced by García Lorca, are favorites of Lehmann's and he must be commended for first having printed Gascoyne's *Gravel Pit Field*.

Life and Letters To-day, edited by Robert Herring, has been very eclectic, interested primarily in what the editor considers good writing rather than in giving expression to any particular school. Herring, himself Scots, has given more space than most English publications to the Scots Renascence and the work of Welsh writers.

Horizon plays a role in contemporary literary England not unlike that once assumed by *The Dial* in America and *The Criterion* in Britain. I do not think Cyril Connolly has been very interested in Romanticism as a movement. He again, has printed primarily what seemed to him to be good writing. With true English hyper- or hemi-insularity, he seems to be unaware of the really rather deafening commotion going on in Scotland.

I have mentioned *Wales*, *Now* and *Transformation*. There is also a small magazine published whenever he has enough material, by Alex Comfort, called *Poetry Folios*. Its most distinctive quality is its judicious editing; a file of *Poetry Folios* would make an excellent anthology of contemporary verse, English, American and European.

William Maclellan is sort of the official publisher to the Scots Renascence. He has printed all the leading figures in handsome, cheap editions, and his *Poetry Scotland* and *Scottish Life and Letters* are amongst the most stimulating periodicals I know.

I have tried to make this collection as comprehensive as possible. In some cases I have had to cut down on the amount of space given to a poet because of high anthology fees, in others, I have been unable to reach, or at least to obtain an answer from the poets I should have like to have included. I am deeply grateful for all the help I have received from many people. To Wrey Gardiner, Brenda Chamberlain, Derek Savage, Alex Comfort, George Woodcock, Nicholas Moore, Denise Levertov, whose advice and correspondence have been valuable to me beyond thanks or estimate. To *Poetry London*, Grey Walls Press, George Routledge Ltd., Faber and Faber, John Lehmann, Lindsay Drummond, Andrew Dakers, and other publishers, who have sent me books and forwarded letters. To the staff of The California State Library and its Sutro Branch in San Francisco, who have been very helpful. And, finally, as always in these cases, to my wife, who has done mountains of typing, and with whom I have discussed the selections at length. It is to her that this book is dedicated, as well as to James Laughlin, to whom it has been a great trial, but who has ultimately always yielded and given me my way, and to whom I, as well as many another, owe more than a book dedication, both as publisher and as friend.

KENNETH REXROTH

Louis Adeane

POEM ON HAMPSTEAD HEATH

The angry future like a winter builds
Storms in the trees and branches in the fields.
The voices threaten in the thickening stream
And thunders frowning in the summer's dream
Shake down the doves like snow,
Turn the quick hourglass low.

The past as heavy as the patterned hand
Moulding the landscape, opens and is stained;
The memory mocks us in its painted cage
And simian gestures on a rural stage
Bidding time's jest begin,
Summon our yokel grin.

Oh leave the dancers and their antic hour,
Prophets with crystals, mirrors of the fair;
The growing present like a tree prepares
These newly branching roots, this storm of leaves, repairs
Gently, oh falling mould,
The loss of what is born, the lapse of what is old.

FOUR POEMS FOR APRIL

I

Now by this lake, this fallen thunderstorm,
Her gold-struck hair is beaten with the grass;
Her limbs lie slackly in the darkening soil,
Grief sifts its pallor on her doom-stained face.

I

My terrible kindness coiled within her will
Still saps her anger with a soothing tongue;
The startling cloud of love, unbearable,
Descends dispersed to silt the struggling wing.

My merciless anima, impending death,
I see your world behind today's caress,
The strangled kitten in the innocent hands,
The dreaming horror and maternal kiss,

And through your candled future I can tell
Our fear-filled present opening like a fan,
The dazzling eyelid tempted into fire,
The transient shadow and the twist of pain.

Yet poise again your love, my beautiful,
Raise quick the innocent child, the smiling flesh,
Lift your white anger and your whip-red mouth
And send your mercy like a lightning flash.

2

Rise from the waves, my rivering one
Curving your slenderness cold and gold
Glimmering on the rocks, or by the sands
Finger the water's wavering line.

There where you ride on clarity
Playing all day with coins of foam
I should beware your buoyancy

Seeing at last that you have come
Out of a whirlpool's fluency
Siren curling a shell of home

Rose as your love's delivering womb,
Knowing the tenderness that I hold
Murmuring always mocks, and in my hands
Lingers the warning bell of doom.

3

Through your grey eyes evasive heaven
Vistas at last the certain happiness
And across skies the sunrise of my vision
Spaces your hair in strands of gold and rose;
Your fountain body melts, the hills of distance
Shimmer to clouds through your transparent pose.

Landscape my lovely dream of hawthorne
Pausing with blossom by the trembling lake
Where the swan glides and poising children
Watch today's smiling image shake
Like unaccountable tears, stay still and valley
Always the curving vase that time could break.

Stay still, my butterfly screen transposing
Thinly the mountains of my view
With delicate wings the webs of crystal,
Veins of your rising love, the crimson dew;
Stay still, my quivering dream, remember
Landscape and future both are you.

4

Gone, my white tangible angel falling
Over the edge of the world into the south,
Daring like emigrant bird the terrible journey,
The swelling exultant exhausted breasts, the
Smiling and bleeding mouth.

Blown with the dust and desires in your revelling
Tangled unsleeping untouchable hair,
Travelling under the serpent and over the reaching
Forests of parasites flowering, leaping,
Avid with arching fire,

Torn, my immaculate angel the tactile
White and gold covering down to the blood
Beating like suns through your beauty, the quivering
Flushing flesh parting, the blood-circles spinning
Staining your curve to red.

Thrown between moving rocks, the impacting
Merciless icebergs sliding to kill,
The blizzard blurring to snow and the soft deluding
South enfolding your wings, accepting your
Spent and pitiful will,

Stone, my intractable strangled angel,
The painted girl in the ice,
Flashing your jewels of tears and swaying
Down in the glacier, silent, gliding,
Frozen for bravery, beautiful.

THE NIGHT LOVES US

This is our love, these wheels and chains,
Walls, windows, vistas, fettered edge of foam.
Our blood blew red and melted; these remains
Are love cooled down to solid shapes of home.

4

Yet outside place, beyond our brittle light
Spread fields incredible, the planes of love;
Invisibly they flood towards our sight,
Our little city stands within a wave.

And growing greenly in subversive park
Their secret fountains flourishing impel
The child to feel love falling from the dark,
The wishing girl to dream beside a well.

So leaping flowers in the burning town
May light the marble gardens of our thought
And running visions melt our coldness down
To fire the insurgent freedom of the heart.

Kenneth Allott

DEPARTURE PLATFORM

It will always be like this
At the unmeeting place:
The scrambling crowds and air
When the gilt clock-hands move
Across the wet moon-face
(Seen cheek touching lip
Through your distracting hair)
To enter time again
Where disappointments live
In shabby comradeship.

All this is nothing new.

Still on the stroke of four
A wilderness of rail
Into which we have come
Feeling like all the lost
Ten tribes of Israel,
Maybe to see and hear
The hobbled tree of steam
Lofting between the wheels
Its paradisal hiss
Under a dripping roof;

The rain still falling now

To share a jealous dream
Of pert and slithering heels
In the rain's puddled glass
Who have the time I leave,
And all the afternoon
A bitter nail, a clove,
A high blind window pane,
When the black pistons drive
Where but away from love.

Now there is nothing new.

CHESHIRE CAT

Tonight the rain sheets down. After an hour
It does not seem there can be any more;
And I am moved,

6

Stripped of whatever's English for savoir-faire,
To tell you, where you are,
How you are loved,
And how your harm I mean if once believed.

Streakingly listening in a rain-darkened door
To roof and railing drip
Beaded like idiot's trembling underlip,
And nervous as a hare;
By a sky deepening like a bruise
I suck the hollow tooth
Of absence, absence until the wet slates whirl:
A syllable would spoil
My choked rage at the between-us leagues of air.

Now the black houses lean
Peopling with your face
My loneliness;
And I mislay the minimum of phlegm
Which furnishes to time
Parodies of what I am
(Oh, scissors and wing-collars of routine)
For all-elastic Gobis of migraine
On a damned continent without a name.

George Barker

I

This is that month, Elizabeth,
  When at the equinox
Biological life divests its death

Equating the paradox
That crosses its dovetails underneath
All internecine sex.

Where silent once, where silent once,
Bedded in negatives we
Held hands across the Winter whence
This April lets us free,
Now up in the solstice dance
We join with biology.

Generation towards generation stirs
Of human and animal;
Prime causes, giving birth to stars,
Gives equally to all
The multiplication of universe
In animal and amoeba.

This is that day, Elizabeth,
The lamb and child have fed
From your abundant hand when both
Begged you for love and food.
The cuckoo, recalling in aftermath,
When he was your performer,
Remember shall in Winter with
Double delight this Summer.

Scattering wreaths the spectres rise
Taking their first deep breath;
The seas go gadding with bright eyes,
Dead desires get up and rejoice
At circumventing death,

And to all these I join my voice
In Love, Elizabeth.

II

So in a one man Europe I sit here
Thinking a peace and a perfect map
Also for the epileptic hemisphere.
What now obsesses us all is shape
Whose horrible mutations, like a birth,
Shed more blood than they're worth,
Like idiot sons. The shape of hope
Is nevertheless innumerable and rises
From all the postures and the disguises
Of loss and defeat and even Europe.

But whistling in the dark brings images
Back that were for a moment on a furlough,
And so my dark is full of mirages
And voices make a birdcage of my pillow.

III

And now there is nothing left to celebrate
But the individual death in a ditch or a plane
Like a cock o' the north in a hurricane.
Out of the bogus glory and the synthetic hate,
The welter of nations and the speeches, O step down
You corpse in the gold and blue, out of a cloud,
My dragonfly, step down into your own:
The ditch and the dislocated wings and the cold
Kiss of the not to be monumental stone.

9

This is the only dignity left, the single
Death without purpose and without understanding
Like birds boys drop with catapults. Not comprehending
Denudes us of the personal aim and angle,
And so we are perfect sacrifice to nothing.

IV

Everywhere is our wilderness everywhere.
I hear the scapegoat's scream wherever I go
And not only from my throat but also
Everyone is our scapegoat everyone.
When by the ilex I lie in the sun
Thinking I'm free a moment, then the crown
Of bleeding christian leaves comes down,
The scapegoat coronation also there.

Or in a world of palm and anthropoid
The shape of Darwin gibbering descends
Out of the leaves of life and from a void
Condemns me to a beginning and an end.
Thus everywhere is our wilderness everywhere,
And everyone is our scapegoat everyone.

V

O Golden Fleece she is where she lies tonight
Trammelled in her sheets like midsummer on a bed,
Kisses like moths flitter over her bright
Mouth, and, as she turns her head,
All space moves over to give her beauty room.

Where her hand, like a bird on the branch of her arm,
Droops its wings over the bedside as she sleeps,

There the air perpetually stays warm
Since, nested, her hand rested there. And she keeps
Under her green thumb life like a growing poem.

My nine-tiered tigress in the cage of sex
I feed with meat that you tear from my side
Crowning your nine months with the paradox:
The love that kisses with a homicide
In robes of red generation resurrects.

The bride who rides the hymenaeal waterfall
Spawning all possibles in her pools of surplus,
Whom the train rapes going into a tunnel,
The imperial multiplicator nothing can nonplus:
My mother Nature is the origin of it all.

At Pharaoh's Feast and in the family cupboard,
Gay corpse, bright skeleton, and the fly in amber,
She sits with her laws like antlers from her forehead
Enmeshing everyone, with flowers and thunder
Adorning the head that destiny never worried.

LOVE POEM

Less the dog begged to die in the sky
    Immortal and transfixed,
Or the tall tree to grow on ground
    Later axed and annexed,
Than my dark one, my sweet stark one,
    Begged the knife in the breast,
The long lie, the lying worm in the bed,
    The cheat I attest.

But bull without a bell I trod
  Among her mysteries,
Simpleton with a bomb I hid
  Shivering in her caves;
And her hand came down out of a cloud,
  Her beauty from the shadows
Emerged and suffered what I did
  To mitigate my sorrows.

LOVE POEM

O tender under her right breast
  Sleep at the waterfall
My daughter, my daughter, and be at rest
  As I at her left shall.

At night the pigeon in the eaves
  Leaves open its bright eye;
Nor will the Seven Sisters cease
  To watch you where you lie.

The pine like a father over your bed
  Will bend down from above
To lay in duty at your head
  The candles of its love.

And in their mothering embrace,
  Sleep on the Rockies' bosom;
The Okanogan Valley shall grace
  Canada round your cradle.

The silver spoon and the one-eyed man,
  The rabbit's foot and the clover,
Be at your bed from morning till
  As now, the day is over.

LOVE POEM

My joy, my jockey, my Gabriel
Who bares his horns above my sleep
Is sleeping now. And I shall keep him
In valley and on pinnacle
And marvellous in my tabernacle.

My peace is where his shoulder holds
My clouds among his skies of face;
His plenty is my peace, my peace:
And like a serpent by a boulder
His shade I rest in glory coiled.

Time will divide us and the sea
Wring its sad hands all day between;
The autumn bring a change of scene.
But always and for ever he
At night will sleep and keep by me.

John Bayliss

OCTOBER

It is now the tenth hour of this October night
with the wind coming in from the sea
and the balances weighing the chances of war.

13

And, as I write, for the fourth year
Mars stands firm in the ascendant
and the sea breaks on lonely stones
under cloud-blur and blare
of an east wind bringing the sound of guns.

Where shall we set our histories?
Who are the errant, the aimless ones
outside the village boundaries,
dead meteorites from long dead suns,
unfree travellers at whose end none stirs.

The meanest priest preserved from dust
wound from wind in mummy-cloth
has more eternity than us
—our character is lost in death
and what are we to passers-by
but grey stone in a field of green?
We have no Arab story here
to bring us hope of Singing Bird
or magic water on our hair
to give us back our former shape.
Unmarried now we lie alone,
a gold ring and a skeleton.

Yeats from darkness drew a tower,
built to cloud and trod the stair;
alone upon a barren moor
communed with wind and star and bird;
from rifled tomb and sacred book
bled secrets till his ageing blood
grew agonies that drove to break

14

his wisdom on the sensual rood.
Aware of creed and craftsman's work,
he found eternity in this,
the wild and dancing turns of grace
young lovers take in the long grass.

Are there not, then, two histories?

Remember Egypt in the Pharaohs' day;
how the artificer against the dust
settling, soft, shifting,
built a sarcophagus to last
the spirit till it enter its new house.
Remember dust gathering
by Nile and Thames,
still witness among the tombs
of life defeated. On diadems
touching, on lips disfiguring,
covering face and lace, sceptre and king,
smothering echoes,
inside door and window deadening,
insidious as an old man's love-making.

Imagine how on low divan
Cleopatra lay, or in great mansion
Lady took lust's occasion,—
silken the sheets, the coverlet of satin,
floor richly carpeted, door shut
lest dust enter on slow foot.
Fate curtained out, cushions, delight
torches and wine taken late
the air scented, aphrodisiac,

for her sake.
But candle guttering, lips grown hard,
eyes tired, hair against gold couch,
drag to the herd. A grey coach
drawn up on the gravel, delight hid
deep under grave or pyramid.

No water-clock or ormolu,
sundial, measure made of sand,
turn for any but Time's hand.
Only myth and legend lie
powerful in the memory.
Isis and Osiris are
sun and moon, and many a star
that rose upon an ancient sky
lives for us and still looks down
with the same pity and disdain.

Here in East and West two armies stand
angering the hot air; their metals bend
blister and warp; the flies reap
rich harvest from the dusty mere.
Here is a cemetery of wire
where tank and lonely sentry keep
the buzzard company. A fire
smokes desultorily.
Over this battlefield the Mede,
Phœnician and Arab rode:
the Pharaohs satisfied their greed
for power and raging Typhon trod
swift upon Osiris' heel.

Weapons made from modern steel
lie above the ancient bronze
and new bodies lie above
Egyptian bones.
This is a strange universe
of star-shell, flare and falling bomb,
where the tall searchlight, like a vase
stands above metallic rain,
and the bombers dull as bees
drone among forgotten stars.
Day and night among the dunes
the guns recoil, the long pursuit
slackens, wavers and returns.
In Gibraltar yellow fruit
hangs ungathered; here lips burn.

Here what shall ambition gather?
—memories of lying together
—English girl, Circassian, Greek,
bead or imitation pearl,
letters coming week by week,
the hopeless passionate appeal;
dead faces, the torn photograph
and here no written epitaph.

Sennaccherib with golden plaque
commemorated victories,
but broken town and sunken ship
and all the prophesying voices,
impatience and sarcastic quip
must suffice for such as these
who die for profit of a claque.

Have we not learnt our histories?

Alison Boodson

CAROL

Fire is what's precious now, is
　　more than gold and under snow
the badger sleeps in peace
　　dreaming winter away.

What's precious now is to lie
　　close-held guarded warm
wrapped in like the ship in the bay
　　or the coal in the crisp flame.

All things fold in all things close
　　together in kindness
the lamb to the ewe, the field to the snow
　　the mouth to the breast.

Turn into me, turn to me,
　　you who are cold out there;
this is the season of charity—
　　come in by the fire.

NIGHT ALERT

A girl awaiting her lover is not more still with fear
than I am, awaiting your kiss.

She does not take more pains to win his wonder than I have
lying here in the dark waiting for you.

All the secrets of joy she holds in her body
preserving them zealously.

I also have secrets from you: you will have to force them
   from me
part of me is still reluctant.

She hears his tread, feels his breath hot on her cheek. A last
panic pervades her, then a long peace.

If I am afraid when you draw near me, remember o lover o
   death
I will be tranquil afterwards.

And now his body and hers are one, the secrets are one by
   one unfolded.
There is no further division between them.

I too will submit to your love; I too will disclose and reveal,
and morning shall find us identified forever.

POEM

I do not want to be your weeping woman
holding you to me with a chain of sorrow.

I can more easily stand the flame of your anger
than the frost of your kisses empty of desire.

I do not want to be your gentle lover
drawing you to me on a rope of pity.

19

Sooner that you never touched me than that you ever
should touch me from a distance made of mercy.

I do not want to be your second mother
always forgiving and smiling and never loving.

If you forget me, forget me utterly. Never
come to my arms without interest. I shall know it.

I do not want to be your weeping woman
pinning you to me on a sword of tears.

POEM

He lying spilt like water from a bowl
   himself the shadow of his own passion
probes with his secret fingers my terrible
   need and sees it is beyond reason.

The dark head laid like dreams on a bare pillow
   once was dreams only but now stirs
under my kiss and slowly slowly
   he wakes and remembers.

O gifts his hands are on my happy breasts;
   he is all warmth and all kindness—
in his long arms I sleep at last,
   and peace is in his kiss.

March 1946: for J. N.

Brenda Chamberlain

POEM

You, who in April laughed, a green god in the sun;
Sang in the bowel-rock below me
Words unknown, but how familiar-strange
Your voice and presence. Other quests
But led .to this, to lie unseen and watch,
From cloud-ascending rib and slab of stone
Your downward passage, greendrake garmented;
A blade of wheat, watered in desolation.

O love in exile now,
I keep the hill-paths open for you; call
The shifting screes, warm rock, the corniced snows
To witness, that no wall
Precipitous, ice-tongued, shall ever stand
Between us, though we rot to feed the crow.

SONG-TALYSARN

Bone-aged is my white horse;
Blunted is the share;
Broken the man who through sad land
Broods on the plough.

Bone-bright was my gelding once;
Burnished was the blade;
Beautiful the youth who in green Spring
Broke earth with song.

LAMENT

My man is a bone ringèd with weed.
Thus it was on my bridal night,
That the sea, risen to a green wall
At our window, quenching love's new delight,
Stood curved between me and the midnight call
Of him who said I was so fair
He could drown for joy in the salt of my hair.
We sail, he said,
Like the placid dead
That have long forgotten the marriage bed.

On my bridal night
Brine stung the window.
Alas, in every night since then
These eyes have rained
For him who made my heart sing
At the lifting of the latch,
For him that will not come again
Weary from the sea.

The wave tore his bright flesh in her greed:
My man is a bone ringèd with weed.

SONG

Heron is harsh with despair
For the felled pine of the upland:
Curlew is torn in her love
For the sea and the hill.

Heart in my breast is a stone
That my man cannot hold me
When hawthorn and plum are
Brave with the blossom of Spring.

DEAD PONIES

There is death enough in Europe without these
dead horses on the mountain.
(They are the underlining, the emphasis of death.)
It is not wonderful that when they live
their eyes are shadowed under mats of hair.
Despair and famine do not gripe so hard
When the bound earth and sky are kept remote
behind clogged hairs.

The snow engulfed them, pressed their withered haunches flat,
filled up their nostrils, burdened the cage of their ribs.
The snow retreated. Their bodies stink to heaven,
Potently crying out to raven, hawk, and dog,
Come pick us clean, cleanse our fine bones of blood.

They were never lovely save as foals
before their necks grew long, uncrested;
but the wildness of the mountain was in their stepping,
the pride of Spring burnt in their haunches;
they were tawny as rushes of the marsh.

The prey-birds have had their fill and preen their feathers:
soft entrails have gone to make the hawk arrogant.

Alex Comfort

THE LOVERS

Across the round field, under the dark male tower
drift the two horses, the chestnut and the black,
aloof and quiet as two similar clouds
alike and distant, heads toward the wind—
and the grass a green pool under moving clouds,
under the sickle gulls, the grey-eyed screaming girls.
Only at night around the standing tower
the stallion's white teeth in the brown mare's shoulder
those eight hoofs fly like thunder in the wind,
like water falling under the night's drum.

FEAR OF THE EARTH

In these cold evenings, when the rain
streams, and the leaves stand closer shuffling feet
the woods grow perilous. They are hungry, the trees,
eavesdropping, sending long shoots to tap the pane.

I can hear you, root, under my hearthstone moving;
white finger, longer since yesterday, nearer
the marrow. In these evenings
the earth leans closer: stones quietly jostle.

I can hear you, under my foot bending
your strange finger. I have heard
cold fruits of my flesh plotted, soft globes swaying—
have known of my skin a leaf foreshadowed.

The captive roses jostle under the hedge.
The celandine is innocent. Underneath
her finger fumbles eyeholes. Every petal
speaks man not hardy nor perennial.

The trees grow perilous. The patient dandelion
should not remain at large in our terrible garden.

THE POSTURES OF LOVE

I

I saw a woman in a green field
Threading upon her hands the bright beads of song
threading her voice among the tall bright ears

and her skin like the skin of water lay
over her body where the light was moving
and from her breasts the daisies dropped like milk

there sang a woman in a field of ears
under a midday heavy as a shroud
and on its windless pool her white song fell

and when the song moved the crop moved with it
and the skyline's blue dust began to rise
the milky flowers in its upright wind

and from the hedges her song called white children
and from the dropping tree above her head
her song's long finger shook a river down

there sang a woman in a field of ears
and her song like bright beads scattered
fell round her thighs among the grass

25

for this song is living, is time—
no virgin knows this song but women only

2

There is a white mare that my love keeps
unridden in a hillside meadow—white
as a white pebble, veined like a stone
a white horse, whiter than a girl

And now for three nights sleeping I have seen
her body naked as a tree for marriage
pale as a stone that the net of water covers

and her veined breasts like hills —the swallow islands
still on the corn's green water: and I know
her dark hairs gathered round an open rose

her pebbles lying under the dappled sea.
And I will ride her thighs' white horses.

3

In the stony night move the stars' white mouths
a net of mouths is looking for food
I think we are their food

they will unlock our fingers, even if we lie
closer than bone to bone—closer than the grave's
white tangled dancers. The streams and the sea will help them

we shall not be able to touch each other
when we feel cold. Somewhere I saw
two Christian lovers waiting in the sand
and round them went the lion, like the stars—

in that last minute feeling each other's flesh
and love whose silence, like the bright silence of wind
washes the trees and islands until night:
till their joined hands sink in a darkness of sand

4

This was Briseis' way: she was a bridge,
a white flute for her master's fingers
he smelling of war and she of woman
breaking her wheeling waves against his rock

This was Milanion's way (the crowd gone home,
and she, trembling to be alone with him)
pinioned his white swan there after the race
and made her thighs a necklace of his own

or this was Helen's way, she, a dark mare
let down her mane, his mouth upon her nape
kneeling, a penitent, her face hidden,
and feeling only Paris in his hands

This was Octavia's way, the rider's way
straight like a candle, her hair a flame,
and outstretched Anthony saw in her half-light
her white horse galloping beside his own

or this was Lais' way, an outspread ship
and he a swimmer on her whitening pool
spanning her hollows with his open hand—
wide opened, like a county or a star

And then the sleep, in various figures, still
his face between her breasts, and she awake
holding him sleeping, listening to the clocks

5

The moon fills up its hollow bowl of milk
bodies grow blue like pebbles in a stream
and light falls like a wind in summer stripping
girls into statues, showing their round limbs
moving but frozen under the watery cloth:
tonight I watch her mask move into sleep
her breathing like a bee on a wood's floor
coming and going to and from the light

She is my field, and in her furrows run
my ways like rain, and the crops of her shadows
are pools, are a wild sea. And she has mountains
stranger than feathers, hard as fishes. There
fall in her hollows shadows of orchard trees
that follow the moon's circle like a tide
grassy nets that move on the dropped apples.

Body, white continent
on all whose beaches break the seas of years
this is the surf they say the dying hear.
We both are islands, and our grassy edge
creeps inwards, like the healing of a wound.
And the windy light is time, a limitless water,
a white sea lying restless as a hand

where no rock rests the gull, and no tree stands
ever, forever—moving, lifeless, alone.

PICK UPON PICK...

Pick upon pick in the sun at the sea edge
the prisoners sing and longer the raw trench
runs, and the hourglass white sand marks their time
and the tide treads its limits, flat as oil

At night the sea falls sharper, the moon fills
their footprints up, and crowding from far out
the waves press earnestly on the streaming edge
of the wire-bright tidemark, and still the prisoners sing

while in their sleep the diggers' feet tread home

Such voices over the wet sand and fields
as carry far inland, restless as a wheel
one long uneasy seaborne howl, the concourse
of voices worn by space to a wordless cry

a shadow of smoke that crosses fields at night
and the sleeping town that turns in its bed can catch
no words but the coming and going hum, the hands
that thunder on doors, o brothers, and is afraid

to hear the prisoners singing in the sea.

NOTES FOR MY SON

Remember when you hear them beginning to say Freedom
Look carefully—see who it is that they want you to butcher.

Remember, when you say that the old trick would not have
fooled you for a moment
That every time it is the trick which seems new.

Remember that you will have to put in irons
Your better nature, if it will desert to them.

Remember, remember their faces—watch them carefully:
For every step you take is on somebody's body

And every cherry you plant for them is a gibbet
And every furrow you turn for them is a grave

Remember, the smell of burning will not sicken you
If they persuade you that it will thaw the world

Beware. The blood of a child does not smell so bitter
If you have shed it with a high moral purpose.

So that because the woodcutter disobeyed
they will not burn her today or any day

So that for lack of a joiner's obedience
The crucifixion will not now take place

So that when they come to sell you their bloody corruption
You will gather the spit of your chest
And plant it in their faces.

SONG FOR THE HEROES

I wonder sometimes if the soldiers lying
under the soil, wrapped in their coats like beggars
sleeping under an arch, their hands filled with leaves

could take vengeance for once on the men who sent them,
coming back like beggars, seeing the homes and fields
that their obedience lost to them, the men of all countries

whether they would have anything to say
as ghosts at frosty windows to sons or brothers
other than this—"Obedience is death."

If you are willing to die, then choose obedience.

"We who are here now, men of all nations,
our hands full of twigs, stones on our eyes,
half-afraid of what we have done (but that is forgotten

a short wild dream, when we were other men
not ourselves—but now we are ourselves again
tradesmen, farmers, students—it is we who are telling you)

you must choose carefully, for your life, and not only your life
will depend on it, in years or days, between believing
like us, that by obedience you could help or profit

the land, the fields, the people; and saying "Death is obedience."

"Because we know now that every cause is just
and time does not discriminate between the aggressor
and the dead child, the Regrettable Necessity

and the foul atrocity—the grass is objective
and turns all citizens into green mounds—
we have had time, as soldiers always have time,

resting before Plataea or Dunkirk or Albuhera
to think about obedience—though we will still spring up
at the whistle; it is too late to withdraw—that someone must
  pay
for all this, and it will be the people.

"We have nothing to tell you but this: to choose carefully
and if you must still obey, we are ready,
your fathers, grandfathers, great-grandfathers, to find you

a place at our dry table, to greet you as soldiers
with a dry nod, and sit, elbow to elbow
silently for always under the sky of soil:

but know you are choosing. When they begin to appeal
to your better nature, your righteous indignation,
your pity for men like yourselves, stand still,

look down and see the lice upon your hide.

"It may be that you, or else your children, at last
will put down your hand and crush them. But if not
remember that we are waiting, good men as you,

not fools, but men who knew the price of obeying,
the lice for what they were, the Cause for a fraud,
hoped for no good and cherished no illusions;

and we will see your mounds spring up in clusters
beside our own, and welcome you with a nod,
crucified like us all, all fellow-ghosts together,

not fooled by the swine, but going with open eyes.

"You have only to speak once—they will melt like smoke,
you have only to meet their eyes—they will go
howling like devils into bottomless death

but if you choose to obey, we shall not blame you
for every lesson is new. We will make room for you
in this cold hall, where every cause is just.

Perhaps you will go with us to frosty windows
putting the same choice as the years go round
eavesdropping when the Gadarenes call our children

or sit debating—when will they disobey?

wrapped in our coats against the impartial cold."
All this I think the buried men would say
clutching their white ribs and their rusted helmets

nationless bones, under the still ground.

Keith Douglas

LEUKOTHEA

When you were alive, my Leukothea
your loveliness was puzzling
and only I knew the processes
by which my ornament lived and breathed.
And when you died
I was persuaded to store you in the earth,

33

and I remember when they put you there
your too expressive living eye
being covered by the dark eyelash
and by its lid for a cerement.
At that moment those who looked at you
wondered, I know, how you could be made
in such exquisite material,
and I would not explain for the world.
Even when they put the soil above you
they saw its unusual texture. The very grass
was a strange plant, previous as emeralds.
So all these years I have lived securely. I knew
I had only to uncover you
to see how the careful earth would have kept
all as it was, untouched. I trusted the ground
I knew the worm and the beetle would go by
and never dare batten on your beauty.

Last night I dreamed and found my trust betrayed
only the little bones and the great ones, disarranged.

TIME EATING

Ravenous Time has flowers for his food
in Autumn, yet can cleverly make good
each petal; devours animals and men,
but for ten dead he can create ten.

If you enquire how secretly you've come
to mansize from the smallness of a stone
it will appear his effort made you rise
so gradually to your proper size.

34

But as he makes he eats; the very part
where he began, even the elusive heart,
Time's ruminative tongue will wash
and slow juice masticate all flesh.

That volatile huge intestine holds
material and abstract in its folds:
thought and ambition melt and even the world
will alter, in that catholic belly curled.

But Time, who ate my love, you cannot make
such another; you who can remake
the lizard's tail and the bright snakeskin
cannot, cannot. That you gobbled in
too quick, and though you brought me from a boy
you can make no more of me, only destroy.

CANOE

Well, I am thinking this may be my last
summer, but cannot lose even a part
of pleasure in the old-fashioned art of
idleness. I cannot stand aghast

at whatever doom hovers in the background:
while grass and buildings and the somnolent river,
who know they are allowed to last for ever,
exchange between them the whole subdued sound

of this hot time. What sudden fearful fate
can alter my shade wandering next year
from a return? Whistle and I will hear

and come again another evening when this boat
travels with you alone towards Iffley:

as you lie looking up for thunder again,
this cool touch does not betoken rain;
it is my spirit that kisses your mouth lightly.

ON A RETURN FROM EGYPT

To stand here in the wings of Europe
disheartened, I have come away
from the sick land where in the sun lay
the gentle sloe-eyed murderers
of themselves, exquisites under a curse;
here to exercise my depleted fury.

For the heart is a coal, growing colder
when jewelled cerulean seas change
into grey rocks, grey water-fringe,
sea and sky altering like a cloth
till colour and sheen are gone both:
cold is an opiate of the soldier.

And all my endeavours are unlucky explorers
come back, abandoning the expedition;
the specimens, the lilies of ambition
still spring in their climate, still unpicked:
but time, time is all I lacked
to find them, as the great collectors before me.

The next month, then, is a window
and with a crash I'll split the glass.

Behind it stands one I must kiss,
person of love or death
a person or a wraith
I fear what I shall find.

THE OFFENSIVE

Written in Egypt shortly before Montgomery's attack

To-night's a moonlit cup
and holds the liquid time
that will run out in flame
in poison we shall sup.

The moon's at home in a passion
of foreboding. Her lord,
the martial sun, abroad
this month will see time fashion

the action we begin
and Time will cage again
the dcvils we let run
whether we lose or win.

In the month's dregs will
a month hence some descry
the too late prophecy
of what the month lets fall.

This overture of quiet
is a minute to think on
the quiet like a curtain
when the piece is complete.

37

So in conjecture stands
my starlit body; the mind
mobile as a fox sneaks round
the sleepers waiting for their wounds.

This overture of quiet
is a minute to think on
the quiet like a curtain
when the piece is complete.

REMEMBER ME

Remember me when I am dead
and simplify me when I'm dead.

As the processes of earth
strip off the colour and the skin:
take the brown hair and blue eye

and leave me simpler than at birth,
when hairless I came howling in
as the moon entered the cold sky.

Of my skeleton perhaps,
so stripped, a learned man will say
"He was of such a type and intelligence," no more.

Thus when in a year collapse
particular memories, you may
deduce, from the long pain I bore

the opinions I held, who was my foe
and what I left, even my appearance,
but incidents will be no guide.

38

Time's wrong-way telescope will show
a minute man ten years hence
and by distance simplified.

Through the lens see if I seem
Substance or nothing: of the world
deserving mention or charitable oblivion,

not by momentary spleen
or love into decision hurled,
leisurely arrive at an opinion.

Remember me when I am dead
and simplify me when I'm dead.

A ROUND NUMBER

The monotonous evil clock
is creeper-climbing on my heart
and with rank ivy will pull down
my hope of happiness and renown.

My sacred lady who needs no art
gives an idiot place to mock.

I know the fragrant girl is dead,
and perished with my innocence
and died two hundred years ago:
or twice that time if Time is slow.

And so reflect for recompense
She only lived inside my head.

Then she is gone, I still remember
my early promise, looking for
obliging fame to make amends,
and here my last existence ends.

For I cannot feed hope any more
and Time has reached a round number.

POEM

These grasses, ancient enemies
waiting at the edge of towns,
conceal a movement of live stones,
the lizards with hooded eyes
of hostile miraculous age.

It is not snow on the green spurs
of hilltops, only towns of white
whose trees are populous with fruit;
with girls whose velvet beauty is
handed down to them, gentle ornaments.

Somewhere in the hard land
and vicious scrub, or fertile place
of women and productive trees
you think you see a devil stand
fronting a creature of good intention,

or fair apples where the snake plays—
don't you? Sweet leaves but poisonous,
or a mantrap in a gay house,
a murderer with a lover's face,
seem to you the signs of this country?

But devil and angel do not fight,
they are the classic Gemini
for whom it's vital to agree
whose interdependent state
this two-faced country reflects. Curiously

though foreigners we surely shall
prove this background's complement,
the kindly visitors who meant
so well all winter but at last fell
unaccountably to killing in the spring.

Adam Drinan

I

LOVE SONG

Soft as the wind your hair,
gull-gleaming your breasts.
I hoard no treasure there.
I do not grope for rest.
I seek you as my home,
that all your sensitive life
may fuse into my own,
and the world match with my wife.

I carry you out of this
to no enchanted isle.
Blood is tart in our kiss,
and no dream in your smile.
Bitter, bitter the hours

41

and coasts of our patrol,
Foggy this Minch of ours,
But I sail with your soul.

I come to you in the flame
of a burst and broken land.
There is acid in my brain
and withering in my hand.
Your touch will plot us wise,
your quiet keep it true;
and joy be the starlight
to what we have to do.

II

Graceful as butterfly orchid
fresh as wet birches in sunshine
bright as the pearly wheatear
  whenever she leaves them
lambs and collie pups follow her.

Modest, patient, as sundew
loyal as collie to master
sagacious as mountain-doe
  whenever she leaves them
eyes of the old folk follow her.

Despite the pines and the heather
Death holds her by the breast;
as surprised, and resigned, they will be
  whenever she leaves them,
as when each of her sisters follows her.

III

Our pastures are bitten and bare
our wool is blown to the winds
our mouths are stopped and dumb
our oatfields weak and thin.
Nobody fishes the loch
nobody stalks the deer.
Let us go down to the sea.
The friendly sea likes to be visited.

Our fathers sleep in the cemetery
their boats, cracked, by their side.
The sea turns round in his sleep
pleasurecraft nod on the tide.
Sea ducks slumber on waves
sea eagles have flown away.
Let us put out to sea.
The fat sea likes to be visited.

Fat sea, what's on your shelf?
all the grey night we wrestled.
To muscle, to skill, to petrol,
Hook oo rin yo!... one herring!
and of that only the head.
Dogfishes had the rest,
a parting gift from the sea.
The merry sea likes to be visited.

Merry sea, what have you sent us?
a rusty english trawler?
The crew put into the hotel
the engineer overhauls her.

43

Gulls snatch offal to leeward.
We on the jetty unite
gifts of the cod we can't afford...
The free sea likes to be visited.

Free were our fathers' boats
whose guts are strewn on the shore.
Steamships were bought by the rich
cheap from the last war.
They tear our nets to pieces
and the sea gives them our fishes.
Even he favours the rich.
The false sea likes to be visited.

Lawrence Durrell

DELOS

(For Diana Gould)

On charts they fall like lace,
Islands consuming in a sea
Born dense with its own blue
And like repairing mirrors holding up
Small towns and trees and rivers
To the still air, the lovely air,
From the clear side of springing Time
In clement places where the windmills ride
Turning over grey springs in Mykonos,
In shadows with a gesture of content.

The statues of the dead here
Embark on sunlight, sealed
Each in her model with the sightless eyes,
The modest stones of Greeks
Who gravely interrupted death by pleasure.
And in harbours softly fallen
The liver-coloured sails,
Sharp-featured brigantines with eyes,
Ride in reception so like women—
The pathetic faculty of girls
To register and utter a desire
In the arms of men upon the new-mown waters,
Follow the wind with their long shining keels
Aimed across Delos at a star.

THIS UNIMPORTANT MORNING

This unimportant morning
Something goes singing where
The capes turn over on their sides
And the warm Adriatic rides
Her blue and sun washing
At the edge of the world and its brilliant cliffs.

Day rings in the higher airs
Pure with cicadas and slowing
Like a pulse to smoke from farms,
Extinguished in the exhausted earth,
Unclenching like a fist and going.

Tress, fume, cool, pour—and overflowing
Unstretch the feathers of birds and shake

Carpets in windows, brush with dew
The up-and-doing, and young lovers now
Their little resurrections make.

And now lightly to kiss all whom sleep
Stitched up—and wake, my darling, wake;
The impatient Boatman has been waiting
Under the house, his long oars folded up
Like wings in waiting on the darkling lake.

TO PING-KU, ASLEEP

You sleeping child asleep, away
Between the confusing world of forms,
The lamplight and the day; you lie
And the pause flows through you like glass,
Asleep in the body of the nautilus.

Between comparison and sleep,
Lips that move in quotation;
The turning of a small blind mind
Like a plant everywhere ascending.
Now our love has become a beanstalk.

Invent a language where the terms
Are smiles; someone in the house now
Only understands warmth and cherish,
Still twig-bound, learning to fly.

This hand exploring the world makes
The diver's deep-sea fingers on the sills
Of underwater windows; all the wrecks

Of our world where the sad blood leads back
Through memory and sense like divers working.

Sleep, my dear, we won't disturb
You, lying in the zones of sleep.
The four walls symbolise love put about
To hold in silence which so soon brims
Over into sadness: it's still dark.

Sleep and rise a lady with a flower
Between your teeth and a cypress
Between your thighs: surely you won't ever
Be puzzled by a poem or disturbed by a poem
Made like fire by the rubbing of two sticks?

EIGHT ASPECTS OF MELISSA

1: BY THE LAKE

If seen by many minds at once your image
As in a prism falling breaks itself,
Or looking upwards from a gleaming spoon
Defies: a smile squeezed up and vanishing
In roundels of diversion like the moon.

Yet here you are confirmed by the smallest
Wish or kiss upon the rising darkness
But rootless as a wick afloat in water,
Fatherless as shoes walking over dead leaves;
A patient whom no envy stirs but joy
And what the harsh chords of your experience leave—

This dark soft eye, so liquid now and hoarse
With pleasure: or your arms in mirrors

47

Combing out softly hair
As lovely as a planet's and remote.

How many several small forevers
Whispered in the rind of the ear
Melissa, by this Mediterranean sea-edge,
Captured and told?
How many additions to the total silence?

Surely we increased you by very little,
But as with a net or gun to make your victims men?

2: THE NIGHT

Cut from the joints of this immense
Darkness up the face of Egypt lying,
We move in the possession of our acts
Alone, the dread apostles of our weakness.

For look. The mauve street is swallowed
And the bats have begun to stitch slowly.
At the stable-door the carpenter's three sons
Bend over a bucket of burning shavings
Warming their inwardness and quite unearthly
As the candle-marking time begins.

Three little magi under vast Capella,
Beloved of all as shy as the astronomer,
She troubles heaven with her golden tears,
Tears flowing down upon us at this window,
The children rapt, the mauve street swallowed,
The harps of flame among the shadows
In Egypt now and far from Nazareth.

3: THE ADEPTS

Some, the great Adepts, found it
A lesser part of them—ashes and thorns—
Where this sea-sickness on a bed
Proved nothing calm and virginal,
But animal, unstable, heavy as lead.

Some wearied for a sex
Like a science of known relations:
A God proved through the flesh—or else a mother.
They dipped in this huge pond and found it
An ocean of shipwrecked mariners instead,
Cried out and foundered, losing one another.

But some sailed into this haven
Laughing, and completely undecided,
Expecting nothing more
Than the mad friendship of bodies,
And farewells undisguised by pride:

They wrote those poems—the diminutives of madness
While at a window some one stood and cried.

4: THE ENCOUNTER

At this the last yet second meeting,
Almost the autumn was postponed for us—
Season when the fermenting lovers lie
Among the gathered bunches quietly.

So formal was it, so incurious:
The chime of glasses, the explorer,

The soldier and the secret agent
With a smile inviting like a target.

Six of a summer evening, you remember.
The painful rehearsal of the smile
And the words: "I am going into a decline,
Promised by summer but by winter disappointed."

The face was turned as sadly as a hare's,
Provoked by prudence and discretion to repeat:
"Some of them die, you know, or go away.
Our denials are only gestures—can we help it?"

Turn to another aspect of the thing.
The cool muslin dress shaken with flowers—
It was not the thought that was unworthy
Knowing all you knew, it was the feeling.

Idly turning from the offered tea I saw
As swimmers see their past, in the lamplight
Burning, particular, fastidious and lost
Your figure forever in the same place,
Same town and country, sorting letters
On a green table from many foreign cities,
The long hare's features, the remarkable sad face.

5: PETRON, THE DESERT FATHER

Waterbirds sailing upon the darkness
Of Mareotis, this was the beginning:
Dry reeds touched by the shallow beaks he heard
On the sand trash of an estuary near Libya,
This dense yellow lake, ringing now
With the unsupportable accents of the Word.

Common among the commoners of promise
He illustrated to the ordinary those
Who found no meaning in the flesh's weakness—
The elegant psychotics on their couches
In Alexandria, hardly tempted him,
With talk of business, war and lovely clothes.

The lemon-skinned, the gold, the half-aware
Were counters for equations he examined,
Grave as their statues fashioned from the life;
A pioneer in pleasure on the long
Linen-shaded colonnades he often heard
Girls' lips puff in the nostrils of the fife.

Now dense as clouded urine moved the lake
Whose waters were to be his ark and fort
By the harsh creed of water-fowl and snake,
To the wave-polished stone he laid his ear
And said: "I dare not ask for what I hope,
And yet I may not speak of what I fear."

6: THE RISING SUN

Now the sun again, like a bloody convict,
Comes up on us, the wheels of everything
Hack and catch the luckless rising;
The newly married, the despairing,
The pious ant and groom,
Open like roses in the darkened bed-room.
The bonds are out and the debentures
Shape the coming day's adventures,
The revising of money by strategy or tears—

And here we lie like riders on a cloud
Whom kisses only can inform
In breath exhaling twenty-thousand years
Of curses on the sun—but not too loud,

While the days of judgment keep,
Lucky ladies sleek with sleep,
Lucky ladies sleek with sleep.

7: VISITATIONS

Left like an unknown's breath on mirrors,
The enchanters, the persuaders
Whom the seasons swallow up,
Only leave us ash in saucers,
Or to mice the last invaders
Open cupboard-doors or else
Lipstick-marks upon a cup.

Fingerprint the crook of time,
Ask him what he means by it,
Eyes and thoughts and lovely bodies,
David's singing, Daphne's wit
Like Eve's apple undigested
Rot within us bit by bit.

Experience in a humour ends,
Wrapped in its own dark metaphor,
And divining winter breaks:
Now one by one the Hungers creep
Up from the orchards of the mind
Here to trouble and confuse
Old men's after-dinner sleep.

8: A Prospect of Children

All summer watch the children in the public garden,
The tribe of children wishing you were like them—
These gruesome little artists of the impulse
For whom the perfect anarchy sustains
A brilliant apprehension of the present,
In games of joy, of love or even murder
On this green springing grass will empty soon
A duller opiate, Loving, to the drains.

Cast down like asterisks among their toys,
Divided by the lines of daylight only
From adventure, crawl among the rocking-horses,
And the totems, dolls and animals and rings
To the tame suffix of a nursery sleep
Where all but few of them
The restless inventories of feeling keep.

Sleep has no walls. Sleep admits
The great Imago with its terror, yet they lie
Like something baking, candid cheek on finger,
With folded lip and eye
Each at the centre of the cobweb seeking
His boy or girl, begotten and confined
In terror like the edges of a table
Begot by passion and confirmed in error.

What can they tell the watcher at the window,
Writing letters, smoking up there alone,
Trapped in the same limitation of his growth
And yet not envying them their childhood
Since he endured his own?

Patrick Evans

AT MORNING AN IRIS

The dead do not specially depress me.
The happiest hour of my life
Was in an Athenian cemetery
In the green of the gold of the light
Of the grass where they grew underfoot.
Something kept coming up through
From their bones, the root and the fruit
Of their past, and the present, and me.
All was one, and as wide as the blue
Aegean, impersonal, fresh, and free.

But the dead do most specially impress me
As some of the living do—
Not only the men and women
(Man is so self-important) but three
Beasts: the bull, the fish and the bee.
For these, like the dead and the living,
Warmer, more bright and more wise
Without learning, keep wisdom of flowers,
The power of a goddess's thighs
(Pallas Athene or Venus).
The fisherman combs out the lea
Of the starfish inhabited sea
With his nets for his bread; and all these
Share with the peaceful dead
In their tombs, with their potsherds and toys,
Their tokens, their terrors and joys,
Their broken and painted memories,
The whispering threat of the terrible seas,

The memento mori, the pleasure of bread
That the teeth cut; the crackle and apprehension
That invade the room when my lover
At morning, an iris,
Combs her electrical head.

GREEN GRASS GROWING

Green grass growing upward splits the concrete pavement.
Who shall tell us of the loveliness of women?
Their words are water, all the fond describers'.
The green grass growing splits the concrete pavement.
No man living tells the majesty of women.

The river flows away, the imperial Thames.
The wrist watch and the alarum clock run, oh, they run down
But no one knows the majesty of women,
The depth of those their bodies, time's soft river.
Clocks run down, but time obeys no watch,
Time stays the same, while fade the imperial women.

The buttocks are an empire and the breasts
Two Indias, while the escarpment of the spine
Is lonely as the Andes. Who loves the Andes,
Who shall expound the loneliness of women,
Women most loved but never understood,
Their sex enduring as the enormous Andes,
Their throats where desire croaks and cowslips grow,
Eyes whose betrayal speaks but utters never a sound?

The taxis dart and overtake the buses,
The colours are bastard and the time is true.
Who shall explain the majesty of women
To us? to us? Exaltation, softness, pleasure.

Gavin Ewart

POEM

To go, to leave the classics and the buildings
So tall and false and intricate with spires,
To run in joy from the imagined wood
As children who have never heard of good,
To feed the flames of the forgotten fires.

This is my wish but my wish cannot be.
At times I should be dead like skull or stone
Or living with the slow life of a tree
Or half-asleep as one would think the sea
Or anything content to be alone.

Not living like this, ticking of a clock,
Afraid of friends and cataloguing wants,
Knowing so little, wanting far too much ...
What else is tenderness but touch?
And what so far from me, though nearer once?

MISS TWYE

Miss Twye was soaping her breasts in her bath
When she heard behind her a meaningful laugh
And to her amazement she discovered
A wicked man in the bathroom cupboard.

G. S. Fraser

SONNET

My simple heart, bred in provincial tenderness,
And my cold mind, that takes the world for theme,
With local pain, with universal remedy,
Avert the real, disturb the noble dream:

And if my hand could touch you timidly,
Or I could laugh with you, and worry less
About the loud guns laughing over Europe,
I might find a local remedy, a province's hope:

Or if I had the hard steel mind of Lenin,
The skill, or even the rage of Catiline
Against the corrupt, the comfortable. Then in

The pages of history one page might be mine.
But for my heart my mind must lose its scope,
And for my mind my heart must give up hope.

CRISIS

My room as usual a disorder of books,
Nothing to my hand, my clothes flung on a chair,
My desk squalid and fussy with useless papers,
I had shut myself up from the clean shock of day.
I was asleep: like a criminal, without dreams,
There was nothing I desired but my own pride.

Then it seemed to me the earth opened,
I was on a green slope, an unsafe hillside,
With rocks there and rivers; there was that lady
And one man, my enemy. We three clung together
And rolled down the hill. The river whelmed,
I gripped her greedily. Then came sorrow,
She was not with me, I drowned alone:
That man mocked on the bank.
                              I almost awakened,
But sorrow and sleep together bind fast.
Falling far, I came to a strange city,
No one knew me, I walked in sorrow alone.
Past smoke-black brick and yellow muslin curtains,
Vainly round interminable corners,
For these streets were familiar and not familiar
(The old tenements of Glasgow and my childhood)
And I knew I would never find my own house.

Then I met myself in my dream, I said clearly,
"I am going soon, take care of yourself, find friends."
But my own eyes looked through me, my voice said,
    "Traitor!"

And I saw then
All the terrible company of the defeated,
Lost but in the courage of shapes of stone:
The stone mouths of the rigid orators,
The elbow half-lifted in a thousand club-rooms
And the steady hand on the trigger turned to stone:
Then I awoke, sweating: I came out to the window,
In the evening light saw the snow grey on the ground.
I turned to my darkening room, I saw my papers

Scattered about, my life too lately
Had been all in bits. "My God," I said, "there is something
Far wrong, certainly, somewhere. But with me or the world?"

A POEM ABOUT LOVE

All that I got from love
Was the impulse to write
Verse for my own and others'
But seldom her delight,

Her whom my verse transforms
As the plain image in time
Loses particular presence
In the tapestry of rhyme,

That flowing tapestry
Where mingled like a stream
All possible delights
And lost fulfillments gleam:

And time transforms her, too,
And all her light would die
But for this echo, this effect,
This agonising cry.

What image is intact
From all that brilliant crowd
But those that wrung my heart
And made me cry aloud?

ELEGY

The waxen and the false grace of tulips,
The scentless heads in many drawing-rooms,
Pursue what I write, like the piano-note,
The velvet dress, and the cake-crumbs,

And the path sweeping up the mossy
Lawns, impoverished by great trees,
And the conservatory's tomato-plants
And all my idle and infertile days:

And you to whom I remain an evil enigma
Remember pleasantly the white of birds
Against the old quad's green, remember
How friendship for us was not upon the cards.

Remember your old coats, your golf umbrella,
Your loud laughter, growth of thought and taste:
And me, in whom your sweet civility
Found only barren soil, a churlish waste.

O lady, had I speech as I have words
And had I love as I have images ...
Think of me silent, awkward, blind,
And wait until the world is at my knees.

I may be pleasant then! Poor egoist
With this one gift, and could but be at ease
With you, who might have saved me from my poetry,
Who offered life, instead of lonely days.

LEAN STREET

Here, where the baby paddles in the gutter,
Here, in the slaty greyness and the gas,
Here, where the women wear dark shawls and mutter
A hasty word as other women pass,

Telling the secret, telling, clucking and tutting,
Sighing, or saying that it served her right,
The bitch!—the words and weather both are cutting
In Causewayend, on this November night.

At pavement's end and in the slaty weather
I stare with glazing eyes at meagre stone,
Rain and the gas are sputtering together
A dreary tune. O leave my heart alone,

O leave my heart alone, I tell my sorrows,
For I will soothe you in a softer bed
And I will numb your grief with fat to-morrows
Who break your milk teeth on this stony bread!

They do not hear. Thought stings me like an adder,
A doorway's sagging plumb-line squints at me,
The fat sky gurgles like a swollen bladder
With the foul rain that rains on poverty.

ON A MEMORY OF BEAUTY

How can the heart for sea and stone
Be cumbered, and forget a face
That moved it once to fret and moan—
Forget the woman, see the place?

61

But was it one or was it two,
Was it a statue or a girl?
Might every spring her form renew
And the white sea-froth be her curl?

Beauty but for a moment shone,
The likeness of a cloud or wave
Whose momentary aspect, gone,
The sieve of memory cannot save.

Right at the back of my head, I know,
Incredible, wild things
Struggle like swans half-blind with snow—
And the dying swan sings.

S. S. CITY OF BENARES

The bell that tolls my syllables can tell
An underwater tale, clang how there fell
Suddenly out of a surface shouting world
Into dumb calm doomed children, and there curled
(Currents' sick fingers whispering at their hair)
Round them a coiling clutch, was our despair.
Sea's soft sad pressure, like the sprawl of love,
Darkly spreadeagled, so they could not move,
The wide wet mouth was heavy, they would choke,
Till in that cold confusion pity spoke:
"This is a nightmare and one is asleep.
This is a dream, my brave one, do not weep,
Often may drown in dreams and not be dead:
Such weight is mother leaning on your bed."

But having thought of this to cheat my pain,
That woe and wonder harrows me again,
Fat clouds seem bulked like whales, while through the green
Grave tons of twilight, in a submarine
Solidity of air like sea I move,
Pressure of horror how our hate hurts love.
Deeper than grief can plummet, mercy lies,
But not so deep as trust in children's eyes,
Justice is high in heaven, but more high
Blood of the innocent shall smear the sky—
Or think that red the flame of seraph wings,
See stained-glass heaven, where each darling sings
In God's dark luminous world of green and gold
As lovely as death's waters, but less cold:
Think what you will, but like the crisping leaf
In whipped October, crack your thoughts to grief.
In the drenched valley, whimpering and cold,
The small ghosts flicker, whisper, unconsoled.

Roy Fuller

WINTER NIGHT

An owl is hooting in the grove,
The moonlight makes the night air mauve,
The trees are regular as crystals,
The thawing road shines black as pistols,
And muffled by the quiet snow
The wind is only felt to blow.
Dread bird that punctually calls!
Its sound inhuman strangely falls

Within the human scale; and I
Am forced to place, besides the cry,
The moon, the trees, the swollen snow,
Reluctantly with what I know.
Even the road conveys the sense
Of being outside experience;
As though, this winter night of war,
The world men made were man's no more.

THE GIRAFFES

I think before they saw me the giraffes
Were watching me. Over the golden grass,
The bush and ragged open tree of thorn,
From a grotesque height, under their lightish horns,
Their eyes fixed on mine as I approached them.
The hills behind descended steeply: iron
Coloured outcroppings of rock half covered by
Dull green and sepia vegetation, dry
And sunlit: and above, the piercing blue
Where clouds like islands lay or like swans flew.

Seen from those hills the scrubby plain is like
A large-scale map whose features have a look
Half menacing, half familiar, and across
Its brightness arms of shadow ceaselessly
Revolve. Like small forked twigs or insects move
Giraffes, upon the great map where they live.

When I went nearer, their long bovine tails
Flicked loosely, and deliberately they turned,
An undulation of dappled grey and brown,

And stood in profile with those curious planes
Of neck and sloping haunches. Just as when
Quite motionless they watched I never thought
Them moved by fear, a desire to be a tree,
So as they put more ground between us I
Saw evidence that there were animals with
Perhaps no wish for intercourse, or no
Capacity.
           Above the falling sun
Like visible winds the clouds are streaked and spun,
And cold and dark now bring the image of
Those creatures walking without pain or love.

NATIVE WORKING ON THE AERODROME

Curls powdered with chalk like a black roman bust,
This prisoner, convicted of a lust
For maize, is whipped to building a great shed
For bombers; and bears the earth upon his head.

LETTER TO MY WIFE

The loud mechanical voices of the sirens
Lure me from sleep and on the heath, like stars,
Moths fall into a mounting shaft of light.
Airplanes whirr over and then the night stays quiet;
The moon is peeled of cloud, its gold is changed
On stone for silver and the cap of sky
Glitters like quartz, impersonal and remote.
This surface is the same, the clock's bland face,
Its smiling moustaches, hide the spring, knotted
Like muscles, and the crouching jungle hammer.

The same but so different with you not here.
This evening when I turned from the clothes you left,
Empty and silk, the souls of swallows flickered
Against the glass of our house: I felt no better
Along the tree massed alleys where I saw
The long pale legs on benches in the dark.
It was no vague nostalgia which I breathed
Between the purple colloids of the air:
My lust was as precise and fierce as that of
The wedge-headed jaguar or the travelling Flaubert.

But I only encountered the ghosts of the suburb,
Those ghosts you know and who are real and walk
And talk in the small public gardens, by the tawdry
Local monuments; the Witch and Big Head
And the others, fleeting and familiar as
Our memories and ambitions, and just as dead.
Being alone they stopped me; Big Head first.
Removing her unbelievable hat, she showed me
What before I had only conjectured, and she whispered:
O lucky you—you might have been born like this.

I knew it was true, but, hurrying on, the Witch
Lifted her cane and barred the way; she is
Lean and very dirty but hanging round
That skeleton are rags of flesh still handsome.
Moving her lips madly and in a foreign tone she said:
Oh do not hope, boy—you will come to this.
I ran, being certain that she had not erred,
Back to our room where now the only noise
Is the icy modulated voice of Mozart
And the false clock ticking on the mantelpiece.

Now in the bubble of London whose glass will soon
Smear into death, at the still calm hour of four,
I see the shadows of our life, the Fates
We narrowly missed, our possible destiny.
I try to say that love is more solid than
Our bodies, but I only want you here.
I know they created love and that the rest
Is ghosts: war murders love—I really say.
But dare I write it to you who have said it
Always and have no consolation from the ghosts?

EPITAPH ON A BOMBING VICTIM

Reader, could his limbs be found
Here would lie a common man:
History inflicts no wound
But explodes what it began,
And with its enormous lust
For division splits the dust.
Do not ask his nation; that
Was History's confederate.

GOOD-BYE FOR A LONG TIME

A furnished room beyond the stinging of
The sea, reached by a gravel road in which
Puddles of rain stare up with clouded eyes:

The photographs of other lives than ours;
The scattered evidence of your so brief
Possession, daffodils fading in a vase.

67

Our kisses here as they have always been,
Half sensual, half sacred, bringing like
A scent our years together, crowds of ghosts.

And then among the thousand thoughts of parting
The kisses grow perfunctory; the years
Are waved away by your retreating arm.

And now I am alone. I am once more
The far-off boy without a memory,
Wandering with an empty deadened self.

Suddenly under my feet there is the small
Body of a bird, startling against the gravel.
I see its tight shut eye, a trace of moisture.

And ruffling its gentle breast the wind, its beak
Sharpened by death: and I am yours again,
Hurt beyond hurting, never to forget.

THE END OF A LEAVE

Out of the damp black night,
The noise of locomotives,
A thousand whispering,
Sharp-nailed, sinewed, slight,
I meet that alien thing
Your hand, with all its motives.

Far from the roof of night
And iron these encounter;
In the gigantic hall

As the severing light
Menaces, human, small,
These hands exchange their counters.

Suddenly our relation
Is terrifyingly simple
Against wretched times,
Like a hand which mimes
Love in this anguished station
Against a whole world's pull.

POEM

Pity, repulsion, love and anger,
The vivid allegorical
Reality of gun and hangar,
Sense of the planet's imminent fall:

Our fathers felt these things before
In another half-forgotten war.

And our emotions are caught part
From them; their weaponed world it is
They should have left to the abyss
Or made it an image of their heart.

SPRING 1942

Once as we were sitting by
The falling sun, the thickening air,
The chaplain came against the sky
And quietly took a vacant chair.

And under the tobacco smoke:
"Freedom," he said, and "Good" and "Duty."
We stared as though a savage spoke.
The scene took on a singular beauty.

And we made no reply to that
Obscure, remote communication,
But only stared at where the flat
Meadow dissolved in vegetation.

And thought: O sick, insatiable
And constant lust; O death, our future;
O revolution in the whole
Of human use of man and nature!

CRUSTACEANS

Upon the beach are thousands of crabs; they are
Small, with one foreclaw curiously developed.
Against the ashen sand I see a forest
Of waving, pink, in some way human, claws.
The crabs advance or, perhaps, retreat a step
And then like Hamlet's father slowly beckon
With that flesh-coloured, yes, obscene, incisor.
These actions in the mass take on a rhythm
—The sexual display of animals,
The dance of the tribe, or the enthusiasm
Of a meeting.
                    If you go closer to the crabs
You see that with their normal claws they are making
Spheres from the sand, small perfect rounds, which they,
After a little preliminary twiddling,

Produce from beneath their bodies suddenly,
Like jugglers, and deposit by their holes.
While this goes on, that monstrous foreclaw, that
Button hole, is motionless. And all around
The shafts sunk by these creatures lie the eggs
Of sand, so patiently, endlessly evolved.

At last I stretch and wave my hand: the crabs
Instantly bolt down their holes and pull a sphere,
A trap door, after them, and in a second
The beach is still.
                    While I was watching them
My eyes unfocused with the effort, or
Maybe it was the whole activity
Which like an idea detached itself from its
Frame, background: and I thought, are these that I
Regard with such pity, disgust, absorption, crabs?

Wrey Gardiner

WALKING IN LONDON

Walking between the ruined walls
Where the stone falls and the dust blows
With the wind from the black desert
Of mankind we do not see
Or do not want to see

I drift with a brown leaf
Whirled by the unseen storm about me,

Leaf in a green world that falls
Long before autumn because the time
Is a dry season of withered hearts
Without love, without the beating and ecstatic rain.

And in my pockets are poems rustling
Like the solitary dry leaf, and a little sand
From last year's beaches, and my eyes
See the images of the real and the unreal city
Floating over the river, remembered
Like the picture we cannot forget
Of the haughty sneering cavalier,
Or the outstretched arms of the crucified man.

OUR TRUE BEGINNINGS

Time breaks our passion but the Virgin smiles
Her hands are clasped in the blue mantle of heaven
And the sea, her haven, is flecked with the white of love
Falling like the reflection of walls in the even water.

For humanity that hears the drum must come to love,
Light leaves in the rain, the memory of night
Coming suddenly over the sea darkening the evil
Of a sad day remembering the lonely evening.

The rails rusted by the deserted quayside,
The ships abandoned to the stone white gulls.
Only in the cold of the solitary hour
We find the crabbed certainty of our true beginnings.

POETRY IS HAPPINESS

Poetry is happiness; and happiness is the shadow of poetry
Like the shape of Orion in the midnight sky
Spread across the darkening and dreadful future,
A cold icicle pure as our merciless nature.

I am the idiot lost on a winter's morning
Bedevilled by despair of the ancient works of man,
Ink on my fingers and murder in my heart,
Lonely as angels or the ghost of time.

Love is my happiness and love my learning,
Words are my undiluted wisdom, not hard my meaning,
Clear as the unseen blackbird singing alone.
Poetry is life and life lies lazy in the sun.

DR. COPPELIUS

Water-still is the shade of old Coppelius,
Winding his toys alone in the empty room
So soon to be filled with the poetry of light
And white limbs listening at the enigmatic door.

Water-silk are the dreams of old Coppelius,
Lost in the attics of all the forgotten towns
Of time, hazy with light of another century,
Only the music now will bring out of the memory.

Days are now dark and dreams are of the dying;
No magic skill is lavished on the doll
With the bright staring eyes and steps like light
Shimmering on the quiet floor of our private world.

73

Robert Garioch

GHAISTIES

Cauld are the ghaisties in yon kirk yaird
  an' cauld the airms
that they mell wi' the mists o' the timm
            breists o' their loves;
at the heid o' their bed cauld angels staund on guaird,
  an' marble doves.
They ken na' the fear o' Gode, as they sleep ayont sin,
  nor the terror o' man
an' there's nane but the angels tae glunch
            at their trueloves' chairms,
yet they lang for the reek o' the
            creeshy swat frae the skin,
  an' the grup o' a huun'.
But we in the warld are alowe
wi' the glawmer o' bluid-reid flame
that loups ti the bluid in your tongue's tip
            as it tingles on mine,
  an' the howe
o' the back we loo wi' oor finger-tips, an' the wame,
brent-white, wi' a flush aneath
            like cramosie wine,
hoo it curves ti meet ma ain!
  O ma sonsie frow
what though the flesh be bruckle,
            an' fiends be slee,
the joys o' the solid earth we'll pree or they dwine,
we'll lauch at daith, an' man, an' the fiend, aw three,
  afore we dee.

(See page 312 for glossary for this poem.)

74

David Gascoyne

THE GRAVEL-PIT FIELD

Beside the stolid opaque flow
Of rain-gorged Thames; beneath a thin
Layer of early-evening light
Which seems to drift, a ragged veil,
Upon the chilly March air's tide:
Upwards in shallow shapeless tiers
A stretch of scurfy pock-marked waste
Sprawls laggardly its acres till
They touch a raw brick-villa'd rim.

Amidst this nondescript terrain
Haphazardly the gravel-pits'
Rough-hewn rust-coloured hollows yawn,
Their steep declivities away
From the field-surface dropping down
Towards the depths below where rain-
Water in turbid pools stagnates
Like scraps of sky decaying in
The sockets of a dead man's stare.

The shabby coat of coarse grass spread
Unevenly across the ruts
And humps of lumpy soil; the bits
Of stick and threads of straw; loose clumps
Of weeds with withered stalks and black
Tatters of leaf and scorched pods: all
These intertwined minutiae

Of Nature's humblest growths persist
In their endurance here like rock.

As with untold intensity
On the far edge of Being, where
Life's last faint forms begin to lose
Name and identity and fade
Away into the void, endures
The final thin triumphant flame
Of all that's most despoiled and bare:
So these last stones, in the extreme
Of their abasement might appear,

Like rare stones such as could have formed
A necklet worn by the dead queen
Of a great Pharaoh, in her tomb . . .
So each abandoned snail-shell strewn
Among these blotched dock-leaves might seem
In the pure ray shed by the loss
Of all man-measured value, like
Some priceless pearl-enamelled toy
Cushioned on green silk under glass.

And who in solitude like this
Can say the unclean mongrel's bones
Which stick out, splintered, through the loose
Side of a gravel-pit, are not
The precious relics of some saint,
Perhaps miraculous? Or that
The lettering on this Woodbine-
Packet's remains ought not to read:
Mene mene tekel upharsin?

Now a breeze gently breathes across
The wilderness's cryptic face;
The meagre grasses scarcely stir;
But when some stranger gust sweeps past,
Seeming as though an unseen swarm
Of sea-birds had disturbed the air
With their strong wings' wide stroke, a gleam
Of freshness hovers everywhere
About the field; and tall weeds shake,

Leaves wave their tiny flags, to show
That the wind blown about the brow
Of this poor plot is nothing less
Than the great constant draught the speed
Of Earth's gyrations makes in Space ...
As I stand musing, overhead
The Zenith's stark light thrusts a ray
Down through dusk's rolling vapours, casts
A last lucidity of day

Across the scene: And in a flash
Of insight I behold the field's
Apotheosis: No-man's-land
Between this world and the beyond,
Remote from men and yet more real
Than any human dwelling-place:
A tabernacle where one stands
As though within the empty space
Round which revolves the Sages' Wheel.

Spring 1941.

ECCE HOMO

Whose is this horrifying face,
This putrid flesh, discoloured, flayed,
Fed on by flies, scorched by the sun?
Whose are these holllow red-filmed eyes
And thorn-spiked head and spear-stuck side?
Behold the Man: He is Man's Son.

Forget the legend, tear the decent veil
That cowardice or interest devised
To make their mortal enemy a friend,
To hide the bitter truth all His wounds tell,
Lest the great scandal be no more disguised:
He is in agony till the world's end,

And we must never sleep during that time!
He is suspended on the cross-tree now
And we are onlookers at the crime,
Callous contemporaries of the slow
Torture of God. Here is the hill
Made ghastly by His spattered blood.

Whereon He hangs and suffers still:
See, the centurions wear riding-boots,
Black shirts and badges and peaked caps,
Greet one another with raised-arm salutes;
They have cold eyes, unsmiling lips;
Yet these His brothers know not what they do.

And on his either side hang dead
A labourer and a factory hand,

Or one is maybe a lynched Jew
And one a Negro or a Red,
Coolie or Ethiopian, Irishman,
Spaniard or German democrat.

Behind His lolling head the sky
Glares like a fiery cataract
Red with the murders of two thousand years
Committed in His name and by
Crusaders, Christian warriors
Defending faith and property.

Amid the plain beneath His transfixed hands,
Exuding darkness as indelible
As guilty stains, fanned by funereal
And lurid airs, besieged by drifting sands
And clefted landslides our about-to-be
Bombed and abandoned cities stand.

He who wept for Jerusalem
Now sees His prophecy extend
Across the greatest cities of the world,
A guilty panic reason cannot stem
Rising to raze them all as He foretold;
And He must watch this drama to the end.

Though often named, He is unknown
To the dark kingdoms at His feet
Where everything disparages His words,
And each man bears the common guilt alone
And goes blindfolded to his fate,
And fear and greed are sovereign lords.

The turning point of history
Must come. Yet the complacent and the proud
And who exploit and kill, may be denied—
Christ of Revolution and of Poetry—
The resurrection and the life
Wrought by your spirit's blood.

Involved in their own sophistry
The black priest and the upright man
Faced by subversive truth shall be struck dumb,
Christ of Revolution and of Poetry,
While the rejected and condemned become
Agents of the divine.

Not from a monstrance silver-wrought
But from the tree of human pain
Redeem our sterile misery,
Christ of Revolution and of Poetry,
That man's long journey through the night
May not have been in vain.

MISERERE

> « Le désespoir a des ailes
> L'amour a pour aile nacre
> Le désespoir
> Les sociétés peuvent changer. »

PIERRE JEAN JOUVE

Tenebrae

"It is finished." The last nail
Has consummated the inhuman pattern, and the veil
Is torn. God's wounds are numbered.

All is now withdrawn: void yawns
The rock-hewn tomb. There is no more
Regeneration in the stricken sun,
The hope of faith no more,
No height no depth no sign
And no more history.

This may it be: and worse.
And may we know Thy perfect darkness.
And may we into Hell descend with Thee.

Pieta

Stark in the pasture on the skull-shaped hill,
In swollen aura of disaster shrunken and
Unsheltered by the ruin of the sky,
Intensely concentrated in themselves the banded
Saints abandoned kneel.

And under the unburdened tree
Great in their midst, the rigid folds
Of a blue cloak upholding as a text
Her grief-scrawled face for the ensuing world to read,
The Mother, whose dead Son's dear head
Weighs like a precious blood-incrusted stone
On her unfathomable breast:

Holds Him God has forsaken, Word made flesh
Made ransom, to the slow smoulder of her heart
Till the catharsis of the race shall be complete.

De Profundis

Out of these depths:

Where footsteps wander in the marsh of death and an
Intense infernal glare is on our faces facing down:

Out of these depths, what shamefaced cry
Half choked in the dry throat, as though a stone
Were our confounded tongue, can ever rise:
Because the mind has been struck blind
And may no more conceive
Thy Throne ...

Because the depths
Are clear with only death's
Marsh-light, because the rock of grief
Is clearly too extreme for us to breach:
Deepen our depths,

And aid our unbelief.

Kyrie

Is man's destructive lust insatiable? There is
Grief in the blow that shatters the innocent face.
Pain blots out clearer sense. And pleasure suffers
The trial thrust of death in even the bride's embrace.

The black catastrophe that can lay waste our worlds
May be unconsciously desired. Fear masks our face;
And tears as warm and cruelly wrung as blood
Are tumbling even in the mouth of our grimace.

82

How can our hope ring true? Fatality of guilt
And complicated anguish confounds time and place;
While from the tottering ancestral house an angry voice
Resounds in prophecy. Grant us extraordinary grace,

O spirit hidden in the dark in us and deep,
And bring to light the dream out of our sleep.

Lachrymae

Slow are the years of light:
                              and more immense
Than the imagination. And the years return
Until the Unity is filled. And heavy are
The lengths of Time with the slow weight of tears.
Since Thou didst weep, on a remote hill-side
Beneath the olive-trees, fires of unnumbered stars
Have burnt the years away, until we see them now:
Since Thou didst weep, as many tears
Have flowed like hourglass sand.
Thy tears were all.
And when our secret face
Is blind because of the mysterious
Surging of tears wrung by our most profound
Presentiment of evil in man's fate, our cruellest wounds
Become Thy stigmata. They are Thy tears which fall.

Ex Nihilo

Here am I now cast down
Beneath the black glare of a netherworld's
Dead suns, dust in my mouth, among
Dun tiers no tears refresh: am cast
Down by a lofty hand,

83

Hand that I love! Lord Light,
How dark is thy arm's will and ironlike
Thy ruler's finger that has sent me here!
Far from Thy face I nothing understand,
But kiss the Hand that has consigned

Me to these latter years where I must learn
The revelation of despair, and find
Among the debris of all certainties
The hardest stone on which to found
Altar and shelter for Eternity.

Sanctus

Incomprehensible—
O Master—fate and mystery
And message and long promised
Revelation! Murmur of the leaves
Of life's prolific tree in the dark haze
Of midsummer: and inspiration of the blood
In the ecstatic secret bed: and bare
Inscription on a prison wall, "For thou shalt persevere
In thine identity...": a momentary glimpsed
Escape into the golden dance of dust
Beyond the window. These are all.

Uncomprehending. But to understand
Is to endure, withstand the withering blight
Of winter night's long desperation, war,
Confusion, till at the dense core
Of this existence all the spirit's force
Becomes acceptance of blind eyes
To see no more. Then they may see at last;
And all they see their vision sanctifies.

W. S. Graham

GIGHA

That firewood pale with salt and burning green
Outfloats its men who waved with a sound of drowning
Their saltcut hands over mazes of this rough bay.
Quietly this morning beside the subsided herds
Of water I walk. The children wade the shallows.
The sun with long legs wades into the sea.

NIGHT'S FALL

Night's fall unlocks the dirge of the sea
To pour up from the shore and befriending
Gestures of water waving, to find me
Dressed warm in a coat of land in a house
Held off the drowned by my blood's race
Over the crops of my step to meet some praise.

The surge by day by night turns lament
And by this night falls round the surrounding
Seaside and countryside and I can't
Sleep one word away on my own for that
Grief sea with a purse of pearls and debt
Wading the land away with salt in his throat.

By this loud night traded into evidence
Of a dark church of voices at hand
I lie, work of the gruff sea's innocence
And lie, work of the deaths I find
On the robbed land breathing air and
The friendly thief sea wealthy with the drowned.

DEFINITION OF MY BROTHER

Each other we meet but live grief rises early
By far the ghost and surest of all the sea
Making doorway to within me. My bowed-down holy
Man of the watchman minute begs that reply,
Your voice or mine.
One another I leave into Eden with. I commit
The grave. Poverty takes over where we two meet.
Time talks over the fair boy. His hot heartbeat
Beats joy back over the knellringing till defeat.

It's a contrary son I'm of. My wave-felled kin
Steal out on the worlding waters farback again
Away to the whirling beaches to reach his alone
Lost eyes and sprinkled miracles of destruction.
Beggar to shine
In once the whalesway wearing the starboard freights,
I promise I'll ship the mad nights to bright benefits
To that seastrolling voice in waves and states
Not mine but what one another contrary creates.

Or do we know a prince bleeding more gently
Away to best the morning at its gates?

POEM

O gentle queen of the afternoon
Wave the last orient of tears.
No daylight comet ever breaks
On so sweet an archipelago
As love on love.

The fundamental negress built
In a cloudy descant of the stars
Surveys no sorrow, invents no limits
Till laughter the watcher of accident
Sways off to God.

O gentle queen of the afternoon
The dawn is rescued dead and risen.
Promise, O bush of blushing joy,
No daylight comet ever breaks
On so sweet an archipelago
As love on love.

John Heath-Stubbs

BEGGAR'S SERENADE

I'm a peevish old man with a penny-whistle
Blowing under your window this blessed evening
But pause a moment and hear the tune I'm playing

I never was handsome and my limbs aren't straight
But I raise my finger and the girls all follow me
And leave some of the spruce young fellows gaping

I had a painted girl whom none spoke well of
And I had a milkmaid who didn't know cow from bull
And a girl with green flesh out of a lucky hill

And I had a lady as fine and as proud as you
To follow me forty leagues and bed under a bush
And I left her weeping at the long lane's end

And are you sure where you will lie to-night, woman?

THE GHOST IN THE CELLARAGE

Climb then by spiral stairways of cold thought
Into the singing darkness—you shall find
God's healing hands are numb-transfixed
By sharp star-splinters to the cruel sky,
And impotent, extended through the night.

O rebel brain, burn through the too-tight skull
Or turn me loose to graze—but then the needle
Pierces more sharply to the unpurged organ;
Flesh is betrayed by flesh, and Love unkindly
Linked to a symmetry of skin and sinew.
No delicate dial is the blood-pump heart,
And all uncircumcised the tender eye-ball.

O you who have found out your love's anatomy
A painful dryness, think of a wounded mole
Working in the earth,
And the poor ghost under the castle pavement.

TWO MEN IN ARMOUR

Stark by the Eastern gate
Stand the two iron men
Full-throated singing

As when before-dawn darkness
Lolls on the Earth, the impossible season
Of flesh subsided or nerves drawn tighter,
The fire-hackled, blood-wattled, needle-spurred cock
Stretches his wings through the blackness, proclaims,

The iron hand is on your shoulder
The iron hand is on your head

When pickpocket water strips the flesh
Green-fingered, lurching the drowned limbs, choking
The pale throat, drums on the bursting eyes;
And rolls and rolls where monstrous things go by,
All selfhood murdered, twitched beneath that tide—

(The iron hand is in your hand)
—When fire filches the proud heart from you, faggoting
Your bones for kindling—oh my Prince
Let music go up then, let praise go up
Like shepherds' fluting on the lonely hills.

Till Love construe the cryptic iron faces.

VIRGIN AND UNICORN

Oh that bright impossible beast of the mind—
He was as wild as the wind, and his own pride
Had turned him savage,
And solitary in his solitary forest;

But my eyes were mirrors and my lap spices,
And he bowed his gold head down, gentle as cornstalks
Under the wind, under the reaping sickle;

And when they wrenched the horn from his splintering skull
He was as full of tears and trust as a child.

89

J. F. Hendry

INVERBERG

Sliced with shade and scarred with snow
A mountain breaks like Mosaic rock
And through the lilt of mist there flow
Restless rivers of pebble, pocked
And speckled, where moss and the centuries grow.

Tree, married to cloud as stem is to feather,
Branches and straddles the convex of sky,
Death is aflame in the bracken where heather
Rears semaphore smoke into high
Blue messenger fire through soundless weather.

Below, like bees, the ivies swarm,
Cast in leaping veins, their trunk, a crippled
Animal of thighs pounced from loch-water, storms
The slated shores of the past into ripples
Interpreting man's fretted cuneiform.

TIR-NAN-OG

A man is born, a man dies,
And in between are miseries.

In between he is alive
But cannot be allowed to live

Since, body's hunger never fed,
The mind is never satisfied

And hands and feet and head and eyes
Are hourly humbled to the knees.

A man dies, a man is born,
And in between a burden borne.

In between, by force of love
A grief in life is made alive

Whose mind is more than satisfied
And body's hunger always fed,

Whose hands rise up from feet and knees,
Encircle head and rub the eyes.

THE SHIP

Here is a ship you made
Out of my breast and sides
As I lay dead in the yards
Under the hammers.

Here is the hull you built
Out of a heart of salt,
Sky-rent, the prey of birds
Strung on the longshore.

Here is her rigging bound
Nerve, sinew, ice and wind
Blowing through the night
The starred dew of beads.

Here her ribs of silver
Once steerless in a culvert
Climb the laddered centuries
To hide a cloud in a frame.

THE CONSTANT NORTH

(For Dee)

Encompass me, my lover,
With your eyes' wide calm.
Though noonday shadows are assembling doom,
The sun remains when I remember them;
And death, if it should come,
Must fall like quiet snow from such clear skies.

Minutes we snatched from the unkind winds
Are grown into daffodils by the sea's
Edge, mocking its green miseries;
Yet I seek you hourly still, over
A new Atlantis loneliness, blind
As a restless needle held by the constant north
          we always have in mind.

ORPHEUS

I shall always come to find you here,
forever among the debris of winter.

In this half-world, this cataract of water
where the elements of vision are dissolved

An ocean pours into the hold of summer,
whose hopes, with ours, are ripped and shelved:

Brown leaf, still branch, sere stick,
the shore is strewn with the season's shipwreck,

And landward through the rains, the sea
unrolls a proud vast tragedy.

Rayner Heppenstall

CONSOLATION IN JULY

Father, be praised for a white jasmine
Thrown over a balcony of flaking iron.
The odour faint, florets quickly discoloured,
It roots in builder's rubble
And the vile, sour clay of London,
A soil for which none living feel affection,
Rubbing it amorously between the fingers.
A skein of brittle stalks, this dormant vine
Yet expressed
White, opaque flesh and the socketed pistil,
The six joined petals and fivefold spears.
Alas, they say
The one inimitable perfume
May now be feigned with bitter almonds,
Tonquin beans, vanilla, that we need
No longer travel to China in our dreams.
And yet I feel with each new efflorescence
My interest in earth is permanent,

93

A current lack of love
Easily compensated in another life.
Nudeleaf, yellow jasmine,
Pale haunters of the winter, potted primula,
Cold cyclamen, the yellow bush that Fortune
Fetched from the heights of lost Yunnan,
Fruitless cherry and the paeony's frilled drumsticks
Promise, promise, when the year is early,
And as the dog-day comes and the parched leaf
Curls on the tree, with eight fingers
Lupin promises (in the anxious palm
A drop of dew like quicksilver).
Promises a late wind,
Tossing the ripe corn to the flying clouds,
And last before there comes an aconite
This ice-bound music crying to be loosed
Promises. Promise all, beyond performance
Unless it be, O Father, by your leave.

SPRING SONG

I have renounced already that hope.   I renounce the
    sudden Whole,
And I will not hope any longer to live my days in the
    clothedness of a vision
Accidents of the numerous daytime so hate.   Yet no
    days live if still, as I say,
Timelessly long, still in the same thought, no more
    untied from Time,
Abroad on the red-bellied bowl of oil, I figure the string
    of the small flame
Of any dark chapel, staring aloft at an image painted
    last year.

I will have patience.   Above all things I will be patient.
  I knelt last year
With John of Ruysbroeck.   And he showed me how it
  is possible for the small flame
Of the soul to be blown into a conflagration that laps
  God round whole,
How the spirit will bound up like an arrow, like the
  strenuous lark.   Only my vision
Is not his.   If I stole the ciborium of St. Catherine now
  and gave the hosts to the Jews as, they say,
Once John of Leuwen, the Jews should prick them and
  they would not bleed, as they would still in John of
  Ruysbroeck's time.

No, I will walk abroad, suffer and comb the days.   In
  this time,
With bounding of sap, without shame, the natural world
  rides out on the peaks of the year,
And in the warm nights the body cries for a lover.
  Now Body is flame,
Not Spirit.   No bounty of God, no supernatural Light,
  no breath of the Whole
Can break through these domes of the hawthorn.   If
  any man in this weather were to say
Other than bridegroom's prayers, the sun would flow
  down out of Heaven and burn up his vision.

     Therefore, I say,
Maximus of Tyre shall be my master.   I will use images.
  I will say
The beaten gold, ivory and silver content me, that
  plants and rivers, in Time,

95

Peaks and the mountain torrents name Him.   The actual
   lineaments of the Whole
Are not present.   Yet I will take pleasure in a lyre, a
   little spear, the particular vision,
A chair, a running-ground, the Lover used.   I will hold
   up the particles of the year
To catch the Light.   I will watch the Most Ample's
   refraction flicker in the small flame.

And, most of all, I will suffer all losses, take from the
   Jews a flame
To leave all my soul a desert where all men may tread.
   I will make out of Time,
Before any host lies steaming upon my tongue, all the days
   of the year
A cataract of knowledges and pain.   I will neither say
Nor see, nor keep any sense from the knife, but at the
   last, without either names or vision,
Stretch my hand out in the close room and feel the Whole.

So I make satisfaction.   Such is my satispassion.   Towards
   my winter vision
It shall be so.   No days live otherwise.   Men must ride
   out of Time
Or get unbroken joys out of Time.   There is no third
   thing   No man will say,
If it were not so, I would have found another use for the
   days of the year.

HAGIOGRAPH

That he would never have any rest this side of his death,
Wailing around the image, Pygmalion,
The many-hearted, knew.   For the joy to relish her with,
Holy as good blue pigments, as lucid as holy things,
Is mastered in one place only.   That is what had made strange
The saint Pygmalion, saint, beggar and thief.

At the gates of cities, catching a dawn through the wild plains,
Wailing around the image, Pygmalion
Scattered out still his many hearts.   He gathered a glance
In the nerve as blue as contemplation, blue as the voice of a dove,
That would shake loose more sacramental textures and savours
   than God ever gave,
The saint Pygmalion, saint, beggar and thief.

This, at the last, was he that baited the mountain gallows,
Wailing around the image, Pygmalion,
The many-hearted man.   And whoever will run into follies
As holy as the morning sea, as the landward flute,
Must cry out for his intercession.   He lives in the heaviest light,
The saint Pygmalion, saint, beggar and thief.

Nigel Heseltine

from MICROCOSMOS

I

I enter and as I enter all is abandoned
like the apple and like the apple
in my hand yet naked

stand and the apple in my hand
slanting on the desolate shore slanting
on the desolate shore. O golden bright
bright here bright O bright here
the light passes in my skin
my skin.

3

My hand cannot smooth your sigh
nor bind your tear, nor scraping mark
your present grave: my hand and yours
unyoked the day, unyoked our year,
our golden eyes' enchanted sight,
and grasping learned the lying frame.
Your grave I know below the roots
of turning pines, your rotted face
I resurrect, your hand and mine
one bone one flesh.

7

He compares his beloved to a snake,
sees that the blossom falling on her head
is snow; she is the calm eye
looks and sees nothing, she
The swift dove and melting meadow.

8

I give you my hand
I dare and I dare not
say yes
trembles my heart trembles
see there it is there

if I knew I were happy
there lets go
I dare and I dare...
I give my hand.

10

Suck the bare sob out of the heart
because the sobbing guts
reach for a life of their own.

16

what, will he come for me
tall and terrible, with silk hanging from his shoulders?
what can I set against his smile?

17

The worm cries not against the storm
the worm that tunnels in the storm
the worm in collapsed ruins
moves among the moss and grasses.

20

mysteries: if a nymph naked and golden
naked as a nymph gold as the skin
of a magic woman, naked as she
lies like a cloud in our dreams:
She lying sighing and crying
at the sky singing and crying
Love love love love.

25

Going to sing about Emily
now they put her in a grave,

she was the buried one
and she didnt die of love.

Now who came to her window
he never came back again,
if she ever saw him,
he looked in and he's gone.

Her yellow box fits her
like they never looked after her
a blowing summer dress on her
they never went after her.

So we put her there neatly
where the scutch grass is plentiful,
and now they've done that for her
That's all we can do for her.

Going to forget about Emily
Because we wont remember her,
Bury her in summertime
And forget her by winter.

32

There are figures like the dark figures
dark three figures in black, they
shadow her they shadow her live
lithe back, soaring I
my eye on her lithe
live body in love I love her
stretched skin and from her leg
so longing I longing I loving

100

mounting eye carried higher her
leaning back tight breasts shallow
breasts breathing I cannot touch cannot
grasp cannot slide cannot hide
in my eye cannot. Three figures
dark figures cherish her shadow her
leaning there, three dark they together, they.

33

In the winter when the wet lanes hissed and sucked,
I walked and whistled and capered in the muck:
I sang Deep River, and that night I would be dancing.

When every path was streaming I splashed my feet
about the floating twigs, and in me was a sweet
girl's name: three weeks to that day
I'd kissed her where we crouched on a dark stairway.

In the dark woods when I
had shot at quick pigeons against the green sky,
I held her to me in a sweet embrace
and kissed the bark of a tree where I pressed my face.

35

I was sat in the church of their Lord
and they told me I was a slave,
and a fat-bellied parson aloft
said I'd a soul he could save;

but I dreamed on a man like a lion
come down from the sky in his glory
of muscle and fire and iron,
and I spat on their Lord's story.

40

Come near me, for the night
brings some cold thing near me:
I am your door, your hand.
What if the boards' voices
come crying as we lay? Dear,
I am your door, your hand.

41

That autumn when the partridges called in the stubble
I waded the wet beet to my knees and angrily fired
at birds who had no part in my trouble,
and blew them apart and walked all day till I was tired.
Gnawing in me that drove my feet on, her face in every wall
her walk upon the hill, her voice, her tall
body below the trees. The hot September sun was like a prison
binding me in parched heat where I trod up and down and
never could reach the horizon

43

I walked the mountains
lonely for you among the windy grasses,
lay like an ear in the night
searching for you in every whisper.

46

Sion the son of Evan sang
like a blind harper in his forge:
I dreaming of dragons in the sparks,
sniff the sharp smoke, and sniff the weapons that hang
long on the smoked walls where carters had drawn hearts.

56

I am like bound because of Abraham's knife
is the core of his heart: my angels are
angels are wraiths are like gone like bound:
how shall I cry when he so holds my life?

57

I cannot dry my eyes when I think of the distant time
The evening was green and transparent behind the cypress
          and pine,
where the rooks flew home cawing and in every bush
the blackbirds chaffered in their own darkness and would not
          hush
till the night melted into the hills, and in the black space
of the sky down twinkled the stars like a gentle loving face.

Sean Jennett

THE QUICK

I

The blossoms dropped before we really saw them,
for we had been so occupied that year
that only death could hold us. And the spring
breathed out its heart in air and fell away
back to the old eclectic earth, and seed
swelled on the naked stalk.
The cuckoo's throat grew harsh
and singing birds forgot their fresh delight
for languid, buxom summer.

And we ignored the change,
even the alteration in ourselves,
the bubbling race of blood, the singing heart,
the reins that thrust in season:
all sounds and pulses smothered by the dread
that built its image in the unknown shadow
and saw in the flowering brake a hideous threat.

The seasons now have taken other colours
by which we know them and divide in sections
that can be the more neatly understood
the confused course, the wild scrawl of war.
The spring is ominous—we have seen it full
of fear and hate and triumph. Summer
dogs with danger every casual thought.
Autumn swells the harvest of defeat.
And winter is the ragged night of sleep
split with fire and the anger of the guns;
and webbed with our intention of revenge,
accumulation of the means of death,
and slow perfection of the secret plan.

2

Another spring grows to its summer fusion
and no eye watches how the small green nipple
spreads into leaf. The time
is only important for the way men use it,
and how God turns his finger in the twig
or pushes a bent knuckle through the soil
is a detail we have lost the care for,
or never known because the years repeat it,
each with its separate tongue mouthing the same syllable.

And yet, we must outlast the time,
we have no choice but to be simple-minded
who must resist the headline and the sponsored lie,
for there is no escape from circumstance
in this live world, important, quarrelling earth,
this dwarf star seething at conception's centre,
troublesome second of eternal time.

3

War is not a dream,
a nightmare to be banished by the shock
of water, or the shaking of a shoulder.
Starting, it will continue in its way
though Christ's wounds gape
and that cross rooting in the bloody earth
grows to the gallows in the conquered city;
and while we struggle now to integrate
custom and usage and the rasp of need
life stumbles from our shadow and is lost
and we know how these years of war
came empty-handed, wolfed, and went their way,
and paid us only the sharp coins of pain,
hate and despair, vengeance and revenge.

The mutilation of the body rears
no architecture for our peaceful days,
nor can the broken or the severed arm
maintain the state. Bitterness and despair,
corroding the foundations of the mind,
will war against us at the end of war
and in the moment of our gaudy triumph
ruin all our gain.

4

Christ taught it at the march of Zabulon,
in Capaernaum, to the eager, thoughtless crowd;
casting out evil spirits from the mad
to drive the malice from the sane and wise:
now in this later time of the tongueless word
when war enmeshes the slow limbs of God,
fight without bitterness, meet without despair
the shock of death; with no hate take
the double pressure on the delicate trigger.
But that loud politician, ranting right
look out for him, for he is totally blind
among the one-eyed and the cataracts,
and his way leads to hell:
not only now,
but, as for our own fathers, after our time,
when the child we have conceived in love
shall grow to manhood in a world at war.

AND THE DEAD

I saw them coming in the eyeless day
in that wan landscape of the undreaming dead,
and they had come so far their bodies leaned
like the thin bent-grass on the wind-lapped moor.
No-one knew of their coming: only the heart
had known, and the idle bones foreseen
the hard bone's breaking: for it ends in this,
the living bone is useless in the end.

O who will shoot the murderer
O who destroy the curse of death

and throw the smoking gun away:
for him the febrile battlefields shall flower
and he shall walk enchanted with his breath.

This one in Libya by the rats
dispersed; this his companion, on the stock
cut in his nick, cut for each silent corpse;
this one in the Donetz, and this in France,
and these who soiled the unforgiving sea:
"blow out, you bugles, over the rich dead!"
The earth is theirs for ever, and the waters
under are swung by their shadowy breath.

Alive they cried out on the other's horror,
charged with unreason of the lunatic
their brother coward, enemy, and killer,
and raper of the cloistered nun and girls
fresh from school. And each to his own banner
gathered from country and from town, and raised
it up for God, and sang their fellowing songs:
and ground the bayonet sharp and charged the gun.

O who will shoot the ranting man
O who destroy the evil glory
and throw the smoking gun away:
though he shall be betrayed and sold for gold
yet he shall live in this or any story.

The evil of that life they know no more
that in their day enraged the shoot of blood
or seared with fear: its residue is shame;
and their hearts are too ashy now for anger.

Against the liar and the inflaming word
they lie protected by the traps of death
who to this commonwealth at last attain
from daylight dream and the wild rage of the world.

So jowl by jowl the sunken veterans come
to this equation: here they are all their own
and like a swallow of material day
have split the hiatus, escaped the pulse
of time, its long frustration and its flare of fear:
nor shall we understand, who suffer still
the thrusting heart and binding ligament
perfection in the final negative.

Glyn Jones

SONG

I kept neat my virginity,
No love gulled me to bed;
I whistled up the mountain stones
My unseen arms outspread—
Lustrous, the lord-star sprang to me,
He was my son instead.

I felt my woody hair pour out
Like water from my head
To see my nipples serpent-mouthed,
My sucking star-child dead.

Lambleddian.

GOLD

A midday half-moon slopes in heaven, tipped
And empty, with her golden liquor spilt.
She rolls transparent on the floor of heaven.
She has splashed her wine of gold upon the broom
And poured it over golden chain adrip
With honey-drench, and emptied it between
My hands where rests the gold-clot of my love's
Fair head, her chainmail cap of golden curls.

Penhyn Gwyr.

NIGHT

This shadow flesh of risen man
Bears on my bones the blurt of pain,
Budges the rock and walks the quays—
The choking bandog snaps his chain.

Her upright body floats the tide,
Fish-teeth pluck cheek-bones bare;
Naked Mary's candled wave
Blows in the harvest of her hair.

Mark the scandal on the hill
Before our feather-raided sea;
Sway like a bell-tongue, hanging man,
And fret your Judas-fruited tree.

The angelled air, the sea is edged
With fever where black Patmos lies;

Beneath his island aching oak
My thunder-hearted lover dies.

Like grief the rowdy swans return,
Rain has her earring on the thorn;
With broken hands I roll my rock
Back on the Pasc of this raw dawn.

Llanon.

Sidney Keyes

THE SNOW

They said, It will be like snow falling—
To-night a hollow wind beating the laurels,
And in the morning quiet, the laurels quiet,
The soft sky resting on the treetops and
The earth not frying any more.

I read it would be safe, like snow lying
Locked in a secret promise with the ground.
And the clear distances, the friendly hills
Would whisper, It is easy, easy as sleep
To the lost traveller frozen in the field.

But now it's come, how different without
Those reassuring voices. Now I face
The bright white glare of January, naked
Among the clashing laurels, while the earth
Stumbles and cries like any lonely lover.

THE WILDERNESS

The red rock wilderness
Shall be my dwelling-place.

Where the wind saws at the bluffs
And the pebble falls like thunder
I shall watch the clawed sun
Tear the rocks asunder.

The seven-branched cactus
Will never sweat wine:
My own bleeding feet
Shall furnish the sign.

The rock says "Endure."
The wind says "Pursue."
The sun says "I will suck your bones
And afterwards bury you."

Laurie Lee

LARCH TREE

Oh, larch tree with scarlet berries
sharpen the morning slender sun
sharpen the thin taste of September
with your aroma of sweet wax and powder delicate.

Fruit is falling in the valley
breaking on the snouts of foxes

111

breaking on the wooden crosses
where children bury the shattered bird.

Fruit is falling in the city
blowing a woman's eyes and fingers
across the street among the bones
of boys who could not speak their love.

I watch a starling cut the sky
a dagger through the blood of cold
and grasses bound by strings of wind
stockade the sobbing fruit among the bees.

Oh, larch tree, with icy hair
your needles thread the thoughts of snow
while in the fields a shivering girl
takes to her breast the sad ripe apples.

JUNIPER

Juniper holds to the moon
a girl adoring a bracelet;
as the hills draw up their knees
they throw off their jasmine girdles.

You are a forest of game,
a thought of nights in procession,
you tread through the bitter fires
of the nasturtium.

I decorate you to a smell of apples,
I divide you among the voices

of owls and cavaliering cocks
And woodpigeons monotonously dry.

I hang lanterns on your mouth
and candles from your passionate crucifix,
and bloody leaves of the virginia
drip with their scarlet oil.

There is a pike in the lake
whose blue teeth eat the midnight stars
piercing the water's velvet skin
and puncturing your sleep.

I am the pike in your breast,
my eyes of clay revolve the waves
while cirrus roots and lilies grow
between our banks of steep embraces.

Denise Levertov

CHRISTMAS 1944

Bright cards above the fire bring no friends near,
fire cannot keep the cold from seeping in.
Spindrift sparkle and candles on the tree
make brave pretence of light; but look out of doors:
Evening already surrounds the curtained house,
draws near, watches;
gardens are blue with frost, and every carol
bears a burden of exile, a song of slaves.
Come in, then, poverty, and come in, death:

this year too many, lie cold, or die in cold,
for any small room's warmth to keep you out.
You sit in empty chairs, gleam in unseeing eyes;
having no home now, you cast your shadow
over the atlas, and rest in restlessness
of our long nights as we lie, dreaming of Europe.

A painted bird or boat above the fire,
a fire in the hearth, a candle in the dark,
a dark excited tree, fresh from the forest,
are all that stand between us and the wind.
The wind has tales to tell of sea and city,
a plague on many houses, fear knocking on the doors;
how venom trickles from the mouth of death,
and trees are white with rage of alien battles.
Who can be happy while the wind recounts
its long sagas of sorrow? Though we are safe
in a flickering circle of winter festival
We dare not laugh; or if we laugh, we lie,
hearing hatred crackle in the coal,
the voice of treason, the voice of love.

THE ANTEROOM

Out of this anteroom whose light is broken
by slatted blinds and rustling portieres,
a tentative room too near the street,
pierced with street voices and the sound of horns,
uneasy halting place of travelling ghosts:

out of this season of uprooted hours,
where time, that should grow round as hanging fruit,
rushes like showers of dry and shrivelled leaves,

and no hour quickens into truth; where love,
confused, can never touch or penetrate
a growing dream, but hovers at its side:

that love, that dream, must travel
into wide landscapes where the heart has rest,
and quietly (as stones, pure on the still earth,
await a strange completion into dream,
by the slow rain, or by a man's desire)
await their transformation into life.

FOLDING A SHIRT

Folding a shirt, a woman stands
still for a moment, to recall
warmth of flesh; her careful hands

heavy on a sleeve, recall
a gesture, or the touch of love;
she leans against the kitchen wall,

listening for a word of love,
but only finds a sound like fear
running through the rooms above.

With folded clothes she folds her fear,
but cannot put desire away,
and cannot make the silence hear.

Unwillingly she puts away
the bread, the wine, the knife,
smooths the bed where lovers lay,

while time's unhesitating knife
cuts away the living hours,
the common rituals of life.

THE BARRICADES

If now you cannot hear me, it is because
your thoughts are held by sounds of destiny
or turn perhaps to darkness, magnetized,
as a doomed ship upon the Manacles
is drawn to end its wandering and down
into the stillness under rock and wave
to lower its bright figurehead; or else
you never heard me, only listening
to that implicit question in the shade,
duplicity that knaws the roots of love.

If now I cannot see you, or be sure
you ever stirred beyond the walls of dream
rising, unbroken battlements, to a sky
heavy with constellations of desire,
it is because those barricades are grown
too tall to scale, too dense to penetrate,
hiding the landscape of your distant life
in which you move, as birds in evening air
far beyond sight trouble the darkening sea
with the low piping of their discontent.

AUTUMN JOURNEY

Out of autumn like a blade
mysteriously engraved, flashes the frost;
stars and leaves are blown to the brown earth,

and burn distantly,
encircle evening in a web of smoke.

Now once again the wanderer deserts
the comfortable myth and the drowsy mansion
where all these months he lay entranced, and heard
the soft forgetful murmur of his flowers,
lovingly bent over their mirrored doubles.

As he looks back, a window lit—
fantastic lemon fruit in the northern woods,
lost in a high facade—suggests
a latent music, and he knows the sound
is both "Farewell" and promises of treasure,
over the hill, among the burning worlds.

POEM

Some are too much at home in the role of wanderer,
watcher, listener; who, by lamplit doors
that open only to another's knock,
commune with shadows and are happier
with ghosts than living guests in a warm house.
They drift about the darkening city squares,
coats blown in evening winds and fingers feeling
familiar holes in pockets, thinking: Life
has always been a counterfeit, a dream
where dreaming figures danced behind the glass.
Yet as they work, or absently stand at a window
letting a tap run and the plates lie wet,
while the bright rain softly shines upon slates,
they feel the whole of life is theirs, the music,
colour, and warmth, and light; hands held

safe in the hands of love; and trees beside them
dark and gentle, growing as they grow,
a part of the world with fire and house and child.
The undertone of all the solitude
is the unceasing question, "Who am I?
A shadow's image on the rainy pavement,
walking in wonder past the vivid windows,
a half contented ghost among my ghosts?
Or one who, imagining light, air, sun,
Can now take root in life, inherit love?"

Alun Lewis

IN HOSPITAL: POONA

Last night I did not fight for sleep
But lay awake from midnight while the world
Turned its slow features to the moving deep
Of darkness, till I knew that you were furled,

Beloved, in the same dark watch as I.
And sixty degrees of longitude beside
Vanished as though a swan in ecstasy
Had spanned the distance from your sleeping side.

And like to swan or moon the whole of Wales
Glided within the parish of my care:
I saw the green tide leap on Cardigan,
Your red yacht riding like a legend there.

And the great mountains Dafydd and Llewelyn,
Plynlimmon, Cader Idris and Eryri

Threshing the darkness back from head and fin,
And also the small nameless mining valley

Whose slopes are scratched with streets and sprawling graves
Dark in the lap of firwoods and great boulders
Where you lay waiting, listening to the waves—
My hot hands touched your white despondent shoulders

—And then ten thousand miles of daylight grew
Between us, and I heard the wild daws crake
In India's starving throat; whereat I knew
That Time upon the heart can break
But love survives the venom of the snake.

Emanuel Litvinov

POEM FOR THE ATOMIC AGE

It is when they come with questions,
how then shall we answer without shame?
Shall we speak parables of barley and fishers,
raise images falsely rural to vex
the candid eye? *There was a tree of evil:*
some had gathered fruit: it was better so,
cutting the root and its worshippers.

It was better so: there were black and white,
just like a game in the parlour.
Only this was played by heroes
and we have verses to prove it.

Once in the war a smooth stranger,
more travelled than Columbus, explained:
Races are different, each has a smell.

Negroes are rank like sweat, the Russian
reeks of mothballs and potato,
Germans of corpses, the Jews of gold
and the gaudy Wop breathes garlic.
But do not the English smell, we asked,
just a little? Ah, I can only speak of soldiers.
The characteristic odour is strong
of Lifebouy soap: it is very good.
And I, I do not smell, he said.

There was another, a very wise owl
with a mouse in his beak hooting
sermons to the broken rafters:
It is a matter of history, someone must write it
and dead men, dead men tell no tales.

And there was an Eye, cold as an oyster,
with the green fire of the sea,
and a Brain like a grey crab crawling
intent upon the movement of its legs;
but worst was the silence whose words
stung like whips and remained unspoken.

Egypt, December, 1945.

NOTE FROM AN INTIMATE DIARY

You must remember this, the cold turning year
when absence was arbitrary and the silent hours
wound endlessly a bright filament of pain

when the thin children huddled against winter
starving the earth of smiles and
over Europe gnarled trees stood bare as crosses

you must remember for it is soon forgotten
how easily a crust can give joy
to birds and children in a time of famine

evil should not be forgotten when idyllic
summer throws bread to avid pigeons
and the desperate amours of air-raid shelters

become once more the white swans who gracefully
symbolised love in the parks of our youth and
whimsical rain spattered your summer frock

to be happy once more is not enough—
one must remember what it is to be unhappy and
how slyly the devils lurk in unwary shadows:

let us not forget, my dear, our December of absence
when we were fortunate still to be alive
even though our brothers and sisters were dead

like Caesar we must reward Jupiter for our luck
and all those lesser gods who are fickle and vain
else will they turn to crows and peck out our eyes:

and one day we will weep so much
a new lake will sail our children's swans . . .
it will be the day when we remember.

Egypt, December, 1945.

Norman McCaig

TWO MUSICS

In any hour the singers with mouths of gold
and fates transparent on their brows like words
trembling out of the mirror of a myth
will trail their sad procession through your head,
in a caterwauling night, in the storm of worlds
insinuating the honeycomb from the grumbling wave
in whose slow sides you see your den of love.

This is your hand, this ivory nest of ghosts,
and this your famished eye whose mediaeval
faith dances worlds upon a needle nerve;
angel with worlds and devil with his doubts
will both surrender them; each to his rival
will grant the space you walk in, and their love
will chivvy you in tribes of another hand
and through the peoples of an eye still blind.

Falseness can never then speak in your look
words I have never heard, nor faithfulness
make its short pilgrimage from you to me,
that will be all my treasure when I seek
in the repeated song your silent voice.
Nothing will change or grow under the sky
but the transmuting myth whose words you'll be
singing and sounding under the grumbling sea.

YOU WITHIN LOVE

You within love are lion leaping in darkness
glorifying night with a fiercer day,
passion of rivers leaping in curled dances,
greed of sun in all the whirling dew.
And love around you echoing only you
conjures the spring in the year's every day.
Bold sun, slim moon
that trembles beyond virgin
I creep with you behind the lion's pounces,
vanish in a morning glitter, rise with passion
in an echoing spring burn every day.

THE TYRANT APPLE IS EATEN

You spoke keys and looked
out of your mind's black book
charming, unspeakable clues
that led my learning eyes

to split the world's ball
and greet magician and devil,
who now make you ancient
and love a century's habit.

We lie in your cunning kindness,
my grey in your thin hands,
quiet as a cobweb, dumb-struck
like a devil in a saint's book.

Hugh Macdiarmid

THE MAN IN THE MOON

The moonbeams kelter i the lift,
An Earth, the bare auld stane,
Glitters aneath the seas o Space,
White as a mammoth's bane.

An, lifted owre the gowden wave,
Peers a dumfoun'ered Thocht,
Wi keethin sicht o a' there is,
An bodily sicht o nocht.

(kelter - undulate; lift - sky; keethin sicht - sight of the keethings or
subsurface shimmer caused by a school of fish)

THE GLEN OF SILENCE

By this cold shuddering fit of fear
My heart divines a presence here,
Goddess or ghost yclept;
Wrecker of homes...

Where have I heard a silence before
Like this that only a lone bird's cries
And the sound of a brawling burn to-day
Serve in this wide empty glen but to emphasize?

Every doctor knows it—the stillness of foetal death,
The indescribable silence over the abdomen then!
A silence literally heard because of the way
It stands out in the auscultation of the abdomen.

Here is an identical silence, picked out
By a bickering burn and a lone bird's wheeple
—The foetal death in this great cleared glen
Where the fear-tholladh nan tighem has done his foul work
—The tragedy of an unevolved people.

(Fear-tholladh nan tighem - Destroyer of homes)

PERFECT

(On the Western Seaboard of South Uist)
(Los muertos abren los ojos a los que viven)

I found a pigeon's skull on the machair,
All the bones pure white and dry, and chalky,
But perfect,
Without a crack or a flaw anywhere

At the back, rising out of the beak,
Were twin domes like bubbles of thin bone,
Almost transparent, where the brain had been
That fixed the tilt of the wings.

(machair - shingle or cobble beach)

O WHA'S BEEN HERE AFORE ME, LASS

O wha's the bride that cairries the bunch
O' thistles blinterin white?
Her cuckold bridegroom little dreids
What he sall ken this nicht.

For closer than gudeman can come
And closer to'r than hersel,

125

Wha didna need her maidenheid
Has wrocht his purpose fell.

O wha's been here afore me, lass,
And hoo did he get in?
—A man that deed or I was born
  This evil thing has din.

And left, as it were on a corpse,
Your maidenheid to me?
—Nae lass, gudeman, sin Time began
  'S hed ony mair to gie.

But I can gie ye kindness, lad,
And a pair o willin hands,
And ye sall hae my briests like stars,
My limbs like willow wands.

And on my lips ye'll heed nae mair,
And in my hair forget,
The seed o a' the men that in
My virgin womb hae met...

(blintering - glimmering; Nae lass *etc.* - no lass, goodman, since
time began, has had any more to give)

MILK-WORT AND BOG COTTON

Cwa een like milk-wort and bog-cotton hair!
I love you, earth, in this mood best o' a'
When the shy spirit like a laich wind moves
And frae the lift nae shadow can fa'

Since there's nocht left to thraw a shadow there
Owre een like milk-wort and milk-white cotton hair.

Wad that nae leaf upon anither wheeled
A shadow either and nae root need dern
In sacrifice to let sic beauty be!
But deep surroondin' darkness I discern
Is aye the price o' licht. Wad licht revealed
Naething but you, and nicht nocht else concealed.

(cwa - come away; een - eyes; milk-wort - the bluebell; laich - low;
lift - sky)

MUNESTRUCK

When the warl's couped roun' as a peerie
That licht-lookin craw o a body, the mune,
Sits on the fower cross-win's
Peerin aa roun.

She's seen me — she's seen me — an straucht
Loupit clean on the quick o my hert.
The quhither o cauld gowd's fairly
Gien me a stert.

An the roorin o oceans noo
Is peerieweerie to me:
Thunner's a tinklin bell: an Time
Whuds like a flee.

(couped - tumbled; peerie - spinningtop; licht - light; craw - crow; mune -
moon; fower - four; straucht - straight; loupit - leapt; quhither - beam;
peerieweerie - diminished to a mere thread of sound)

THE EEMIS-STANE

I' the how-dumb-deid o the cauld hairst nicht
The warl like an eemis-stane
Wags i the lift;
An my eerie memories fa'
Like a yowdendrift.

Like a yowdendrift so's I couldna read
The words cut oot i the stane
Had the fug o fame
An history's hazelraw
No' yirdit thaim.

(how-dumb-deid - "the dead of night"; hairst - harvest-autumn; warl
- world; eemis-stane - tiltingrock; lift - sky; yowendrift - swirl of snow;
fug - moss; hazelraw - lichen)

THE WATERGAW

Ae weet forenicht i the yow-trummle
I saw yon antrin thing.
A watergaw wi its chitterin licht
Ayont the on-ding;
An I thocht o the last wild look ye gied
Afore ye deed!

There was nae reek i the laverock's hoose
That nicht-an nane i mine;
But I hae thocht o that foolish licht
Ever sin syne;
An I think that mebbe at last I ken
What your look meant then.

(weet - wet; yow-trummle - ewe-tremble: a cold spell after sheep shearing;
antrin - rare; watergaw - rainbow; chitterin - shivering; ayont - against;
on-ding - downpour; reek - smoke; laverock's - lark's; hoose - house)

IN THE HEDGEBACK

It was a wild black nicht,
But i the hert o't we
Drave back the darkness wi a bleeze o licht,
Ferrer than een could see.

It was a wild black nicht,
But o the snell air we
Kept juist eneuch to hinder the heat
Meltin us utterly.

It was a wild black nicht,
But o the win's roar we
Kept juist eneuch to hear oor herts beat
Owre it triumphantly.

It was a wild black nicht,
But o the Earth we
Kept juist eneuch underneath us to ken
That a warl used to be.

(snell - bitter cold)

Sorley Maclean

(from his own Gaelic)

KNIGHTSBRIDGE OF LIBYA   *(June, 1942)*

Though I am to-day against the breast of battle, not here my
burden and extremity; not Rommel's guns and tanks, but that
my darling should be crooked and a liar.

129

TO A DEPRAVED LYING WOMAN

If I were dead in the Desert—as you would like me to be—would not your lies be luxuriant, many-coloured on my corpse. For every grain of dry sand choking my mouth and eye, you would have a lie to match it—Himeimat would not be such a pile. There would not be a corpse between El Ragil and bloody Eleut El Tamar who would not prefer as clothing his load of sand to your nimble lie. After your adultery and Nancy-boy who misled you with his warm money, your ready lie would put a cloak over the sordidness of your vicissitudes.

THE NIGHTMARE

One night of the two bad years when I thought my love was maimed with a hurt as bad as woman has had since Eve's generation, we were together in a dream beside the stone wall that is between the boys' and girls' playgrounds of my first school; she was in my arms and my mouth was going to her lips when the loathsome head started suddenly from behind the wall; and the long foul dim fingers seized my throat in a sudden grip, and the words of despair followed: Too late, you fool.

from DAIN EILE

My eye is not on Calvary, nor on Bethlehem the Blessed, but on a foul-smelling backland in Glasgow, where life rots as it grows; and on a room in Edinburgh, a room of poverty and pain, where the diseased infant writhes and wallows till death.

from DAIN do EIMHIR

XVII

Multitude of the skies, gold riddle of millions of stars, cold, distant, lustrous, beautiful, silent, unconscious, unwelcoming.

Fullness of knowledge in their course, emptiness of chartless ignorance, a universe moving in silence, a mind alone in its bounds.

Not they moved my thoughts, not the marvel of their chill course; to us there is no miracle but in love, lighting of a universe in the kindling of your face.

XIX

I gave you immortality and what did you give me? Only the sharp arrows of your beauty, a harsh onset and piercing sorrow, bitterness of spirit and a sore gleam of glory.

If I gave you immortality you gave it to me; you put an edge on my spirit and radiance in my song. And though you spoiled my understanding of the conflict, yet, were I to see you again, I should accept more and the whole of it.

Were I, after oblivion of my trouble, to see before me on the plain of the land of youth the gracious form of your beauty, I should prefer it there, although my weakness would return, and to peace of spirit again to be wounded.

O yellow-haired, lovely girl, you tore my strength and inclined my course from its aim: but, if I reach my place, the high wood of the men of song, you are the fire of my lyric—you made a poet of me through sorrow.

I raised this pillar on the shifting mountain of time, but it is a memorial-stone that will be heeded till the Deluge, and, though you will be married to another and ignorant of my struggle, your glory is my poetry, after the slow rotting of your beauty.

XXII

I walked with my reason out beside the sea: we were together but it kept a little distance from me.

Then it turned saying: Is it true you heard that your fair love is marrying early on Monday?

I checked the heart that rose in my torn, swift breast and said: most likely, why should I lie?

How should I think I would seize the radiant golden star, that I could catch it and put it prudently in my pocket?

I did not take a cross's death in the sore extremity of Spain, and how then should I expect the one new gift of fate?

I followed only a way that was small, mean, low, dry, and lukewarm: and how then should I meet the thunderbolt of love?

But had I the choice again, and stood on that headland, I should leap from heaven or hell with a whole spirit and heart.

XXX

A Bolshevik who never gave heed to queen or to king, yet, had we Scotland free, Scotland equal to our love, a white, spirited, generous Scotland, without petty, paltry, vapid bourgeoisie, without the loathesomeness of capitalists, without hateful, crass graft, the mettlesome Scotland of the free, the Scotland of our blood, the Scotland of our love, I would break the legitimate law of the kings, I would break the sure law of the wise, I would proclaim you queen of Scotland in spite of the new republic.

LIV

You were dawn on the Cuillin and benign day on the Clarach, the sun on his elbows in the golden stream and the white rose that breaks the horizon.

Glitter of sails on a sunlit firth, blue of the ocean and aureate sky, the young morning in your head of hair and in your clear lovely cheeks.

My jewel of dawn and night your face and beloved kindness, though with the grey shaft of grief my young morning is transfixed.

LV

I do not see the sense of my toil putting thoughts in a dying tongue, now when the whoredom of Europe is murder erect and agony: but we have been given a million years, a fragment of a sad, growing portion, the courage and patience of the many and the marvel of a beautiful face.

Joseph Gordon Macleod

From THE ECLIPTIC: CANCER, or, THE CRAB

Moonpoison, mullock of sacrifice,
Suffuses the veins of the eyes
Till the retina, mooncoloured,
Sees the sideways motion of the cretin crab
Hued thus like a tortoise askew in the glaucous moonscape
A flat hot boulder it
Lividly in the midst of the Doldrums
Sidles
The lunatic unable to bear the silent course of constellations
Mad and stark naked
Sidles
The obol on an eyeball of a man dead from elephantiasis
Sidles
All three across heaven with a rocking motion.
The Doldrums: "region of calms and light baffling winds
near Equator."

But the calms are rare
The winds baffling but not light
And the drunken boats belonging to the Crab Club
Rock hot and naked to the dunning of the moon
All in the pallescent Sargasso weed
And windbound, seeking distraction by the light of deliverance
For
What are we but the excrement of non-existent noon?
  (Truth like starlight crookedly)
What are we all but "burial grounds abhorred by the moon?"

And did the Maoris die of measles? So do we.

But there is no snow here, nor lilies.
The night is glutinous
In a broad hearth crisscross thorn clumps
Smoulder: distant fireback of copse
Throws back silence: glassen ashes gleam in pond
The constellations which have stopped working (?)
Shimmer. No dead leaf jumps.
On edge of lawn a glowworm
Hangs out its state-recognized torchlamp
Blocks of flowers gape dumb as windows with blinds drawn
And in the centre the rugate trees
Though seeming as if they go up in smoke
Are held like cardboard where they are.
Bluehot it is queer fuel to make the moon move.

Agesias said: "Nero was an artist because he murdered his
    mother
Sensibility (subliminal) is of more importance than moral
    obligation (prandial)."
But Agesias paints cottages in watercolours and fears his
    own mother
Barbaricus said: "I am passionately in love with Gito who
    spurns me for Prainoê"
But until he saw them together he was merely disturbed by
    Gito's eyelashes
Galônus said: "The subsequent shrivelling of an orchid doesn't
    alter the value of its beauty."
Decanus said: "Joy in nothing. Either dies joy or what
    produced it."

But Galônus is attractive to women, Decanus obese, poor,
    obtuse.

Epinondas said: "I have been a liar, now no longer so."
Zeuxias said: "What I have always been, I shall remain, a fool."
Is it better to be self-deceived or lazy?
Epator was drunk for two days: Theodorus traced his disease
  to college, Iphogenês saw God and died,
And so down the Alphabet, aye, and the Persian,
With variegated gutturals and sibilants, the Gaelic with
  diphthongs and triphthongs,
Choctaw with three different clicks
Each letter is somebody
But the Crab is nobody
Nobody
Nobody
A ganglion of neurotic imitations
Composed of each letter in turn
Jointed by conflicts he does not want
A word that never existed with a sense nobody can understand.
Suffering for the sins his father refused to commit
He sits and thinks about the twiddling toes of Gunerita
A boy-girl or girl-boy of an average pulchritude
Haunted by phantoms of his female self
        Whom he was never seen but composed himself, thus:
        Breasts of Augustina brains of Beatrice
        Arms of Capucine on the motherliness of Dorothea
        Eyes of Evelyn in the brow of Francesca
        Fragrance of Gretchen with the understanding of Helen
This he desires, but despises:
Bhah!
Always sideways, crabs walk.

Either he is not fit for this world
Or this world not fit for him. But which?

After all this pain of development is there neither interval
   nor reward?
They lured him with promises,
Now it has all slipped sideways
What is the good, I ask you, of going into a melting-pot
If fated to melt again after getting out of it?
The answers are: He is not out of it
Determined to budge not from yon slippery rock
Not a yard, no, nor an inch, no, nor a barleycorn's breadth
For chance is not blind but unimpedable
And we call it blind because
Since we frustrate it only by chance
We prefer to shut our own eyes.

The crab however crawls on.

He must therefore be a crab subnormal.
One day, one of his foreclaws, assembled as usual by many
   men,
Being longer than the other, turns and pinches his tentacles
With the other he pinches the persons that assembled the
   long one
Next day the short one, equally alien, is the longer
And the process is reversed.
In mass production one hand never knows
The evil the other is inspiring it to do
This is a heretic even to the faiths he fails to believe
So worthless, awkward, unintelligible,
The crab crawls on.

He has suffered because he was ugly
Let him be cruel now that he is attractive

137

Caring not whether he fructifies cruelty or is merely hard on self.
We trap our goldfinch trapping our souls therewinged
Sacrifice our mad gods to the madder gods:
We hymn the two sons of Leda and Zeus-Aegis-bearer
We don't. We drink and drivel. My
poor Catullus, do stop being such a
Fool. Admit that lost which as you watch is
gone. O, once the days shone very bright for
you, when where that girl you loved so (as no
other will be) called, you came and came. And
then and there were odd things done and many
which you wanted and she didn't not want.
Yes indeed the days shone very bright for
you. But now she doesn't want it.
                              Don't you either,
booby. Don't keep chasing her. Don't live in
misery, carry on, be firm, be hardened.
Goodbye, girl: Catullus is quite hardened,
doesn't want you, doesn't ask, if you're not
keen— though sorry you'll be to be not asked.
Yes, poor sinner... what is left in life for
you? Who'll now go with you? Who'll be attracted?
Whom'll you love now? Whom say you belong to?
Whom'll you now kiss? Whose lips'll you nibble?
—Now you, Catullus! you've decided to be hardened.

How can I be hardened when the whole world is fluid?
O Aphroditê Pandêmos, your badgers rolling in the moonlit
corn

Corn blue-bloom-covered carpeting the wind
Wind humming like distant rooks
Distant rooks busy like factory whirring metal

138

Whirring metallic starlings bizarre like cogwheels missing teeth
These last grinning like the backs of old motor cars
Old motor cars smelling of tragomaschality
Tragomaschality denoting the triumph of self over civilization
Civilization being relative our to Greek
      Greek to Persian
      Persian to Chinese
Chinese politely making borborygms to show satisfaction
Satisfaction a matter of capacity
Capacity not significance: otherwise with an epigram
Epigrams— poems with a strabismus
Strabismus being as common spiritually as optically the moon
The moon tramping regular steps like a policeman past the
  houses of the Zodiac
And the Zodiac itself, whirling and flaming sideways
Circling from no point returning through no point
Endlessly skidding as long as man skids, though never moving,
Wavers, topples, dissolves like a sandcastle into acidity.

Is there nothing more soluble, more gaseous, more imper-
  ceptible?
Nothing.

Charles Madge

IN CONJUNCTION

Now in the circulating torrent of the stars
Certain events are drawn correct and clear
Faces that wear expressions of anguish and delight

Signs unmistakable of the heavenly progress
The flying planet leaves the night house
The two twined figures fill the highest hemisphere

From which we conclude peace, and grateful offerings
While the bird of war, thunderless on leaden roof
No shadow shows on the galactic brilliance of the streaming
  breast

And beyond the fated, tragic, foursquare, immovable house
Evenings under trees of calm, descending evening of rest
Relenting over battlefields, evenings upholding us
Among alarms, rust and the dead, waiting to be blest.

THE BIRDS OF TIN

The birds of tin
We cannot eat.

We play with them
They cost us nothing
The birds of tin
Municipal

They fly, they float
They wave to us
From far away
They come to rest
Perfectly flat
      medals
Of innumerable sizes
On the surface of the sea.
Some are enormously large
Some are six feet high
Some you can hold
Some you can put in your mouth

Some slip through your fingers
And there are microscopic
   tiny birds.
In vain we speak to them
In vain we call to them
Or entreat them to open their wings.
They are affixed to walls
Pinned to the sky
Attached by screws
Tied by chains
The birds of tin
Are dead.

DELUSIONS VI

Without surprise, on that not distant shore
Wandering feet mounting towards the trees
A pilgrim guide, until, just as before
The infant brook and half-hid house he sees.

The same, the inarticulate music moves
Depending foliage of annual green
And mutters through the fastness of his groves
Meaningless comment on the well-known scene.

He listens, ears pricked up, and strains his eyes
On to the polar image of his heart.
A retina matured with other skies
Receives the impressions that the woods impart.

Oh wanderer, do not turn back your feet
To the green haunt and the imprisoned wood.
Enough that trickling streams ever repeat
Their senseless noise to perfect solitude.

A NIGHTLY DEED

Sir, the night is darker now
  And the wind blows stronger,
Fails my heart I know not how
  I can go no longer.

Spectres rise on every side,
  Spectres of the Brocken,
With their bony arms out wide
  I can see them mocking.

Empty as an old tin can
  Is each horrid phantom,
Neither ghost they are nor man,
  I can't understand 'em.

If Napoleon's in his grave
  And Bruin in the mountain,
This must be the ocean wave
  Roaring in the fountain.

Eyes no eyes but drops of lead
  Pennies and a farthing,
There is nothing to be said,
  But the poor man starving.

See his cold and empty grate,
  See his little cottage,
See his cold and empty plate,
  He has got no pottage.

Sir the night is darker now,
    And the wind blows cruel,
Let us go, I know not how,
    And fetch him winter fuel.

RUMBA OF THE THREE LOST SOULS

Cold and holy oak
Hear the raven croak:
The policeman's helmet
    Has bewitched our feet.

The helmet on the stalk
Is the way that we walk
And we sit, having dived,
    Fully dressed, on the seat.

Here together where we fell
By the merman's well
In the light of the trees
    Of the dead man's street.

Undivided are we
Numbers one two and three
We were let down
    By the knotted sheet.

Rhythm beyond control
Is the lot of each soul
And because we fell together
    Here again we meet.

The wizard in the yard
Took the heart that was hard.
Not all Scotland can recall
    What the eagles eat.

TO MAKE A BRIDGE

To make a bridge
Between poetry and prose

To make a movable bridge
Between this year and next year

To know the male from the female embryo
By auscultation

To enable the plotting of barometric areas

To make a bridge
Between heaven and earth

To make a bridge
Between man and man
And between men and men
A bridge across the grey dividing river
A skeleton bridge
(Their bones fly electrically
To arch themselves in a system of stresses
Exactly and patiently
Between the lines of the two camps)

A flying bridge
In the dark air
Sensible of the currents

A bridge between you and me

To make such a bridge
Foresight and cunning
The development of additional organs

In peace
The building of new brains
Lobe by lobe
In the wide spaces and the free pathways of the wind

The collection of materials
The sorting of minerals
The naming of substances
The enumeration of all these
And the congratulation of all those
Who live in a certain part of a certain place

The co-ordinates of pleasure

In the category of bridges
We have this bridge and that bridge
But whatever the bridge
And wherever the bridge
There is only one space
Hungry, roaring and indivisible
Under the bridge

To be kind to each other
To help in construction
To be sorry
To be aware of the difficulties
To give treatment
To arrange food supplies
To make shelters and centres for the construction of bridges
To allow time
To put together and to take to pieces
Talking quietly and thinking loudly
We have undertaken.

Os Marron

NOCTURNAL

The roof of midnight, hushed and high;
covers the house in silence deep; then I
hear laughter from my daughter in her sleep.

So gay a laugh yet
like a folk song hung from the secret
melancholy thread holding all happiness.
I know that summer has facades disturbed
like curtains on a stage by small winds of sadness
blossom in joy lets fall a white tear
the curving moon can be a scimitar
roses are barbed.
                    So must her dreams be.
Her girlish light must scale the cliff of sleep
by paths unimagineably pure.
                    O sea
forgo this dreamer, for her dear gold
I covet; her daylight laughter caught so lovingly
in sleep slips like light into dark water
to a desperate fathom.
                    So must her dreams be . . .

William Montgomerie

ELEGY FOR WILLIAM SOUTAR

A narrowing of knowledge to one window to a door
Swinging inward on a man in a windless room
On a man inwardly singing
                              on a singing child
Alone and never alone a lonely child
Singing
        in a mirror dancing to a dancing child
Memory sang and words in a mimic dance
Old words were young and a child sang.

A narrowing of knowledge to one room to a doorway
To a door in a wall swinging bringing him friends
A narrowing of knowledge to
                              an arrow in bone in the marrow
An arrow
          death
                  strung on the string of the spine.

To the live crystal in the palm and the five fingers
To the slow thirty years' pearl in the hand
Shelled in a skull in the live face of a statue
Sea-flowered on the neck of broken marble
Sunken fourteen years in that aquarium.

Nicholas Moore

WINTER AND RED BERRIES

Come, put off your gown of smooth lilac,
And whisper your intricacies to winter.
The snow will have a better ear than I
For all that lovers say—red heresies!

How can I be a heretic? How can
I who am man be any other thing?
My answer is compounded of sad guns
Answering other guns with sounds as sad,

And these repeat the questions of the last.
My dear, the time for murmurings is past.
Here come the conquerors, here tread the beasts,
Wolves, antelopes fleeing before the wind,

And nothing I can say will now be kind!
Befriend the wolf, befriend the stricken deer,
Befriend the camel and the shy tapir,
These animals are lovelier than...

O yet strip off your lilac gown,
Whisper and sing, and I will slide between
Your hands like so much sand: like so much wine
The bouquet of your flesh turn sad by mine.

THE HAIR'S-BREADTH

(For Priscilla)

Tell me, hair of her head, where I should lie
Who wish to praise her in my poetry?
Tell me, hair of her thigh, what I should do
Who wish to make my image of her true?

Dog by the lamp-post, God above the clouds,
Am I to follow either with my words?
Is she a bitch to be by flesh accosted,
Or holy image and by blood attested?

Tell me, hair of her whole anatomy,
With what attentions I may make her happy?
Tell me, hair of her heart, what I can be
To tender her in all world's misery?

The blood of love may flow from me to her,
But how can I describe it by a hair?

FRED APOLLUS AT FAVA'S

My sexual feats—
It is accounts of these
Each friend entreats.
They do not care what women wear or what artistic fashion
  meets
My best approval.
Love is all.

149

There are no swans
But Leda's, and its hiss,
Majestic once,
Grows tame with telling over tea and the inevitable buns.
They hate Picasso—
Art's no go.

They only like the rude
Reclining nude
The shiny-covered magazines all show,
This svelte form,
The velvet norm
Of their romantic discipline,
Whose wild imaginations flow
Towards flesh more bright than I have ever seen.

And am I like a god
Who sit and nod
At their remarks? Experienced in all
The ways of love,
Each subtle move?
I hate them as their hard words rise
Over their plates of pork and fall
Against my ear. They take me by surprise;

For, suddenly, I know myself a jealous man,
An also-ran
Unfit to face the company of such,
Who obviously touch
Such transports of delight as I
Have never known. How can I qualify?

It only seems I have my dreams and hopes,
      Those bitter shapes
Of unloved breasts and thighs that pass,
      (Each one my golden ass!)—
My sexual feats are all my friends',
Not mine. Not me to whom the red tongue sends

      Such thrills.
(It is the thought that kills!)

      These men
(How vainly!) turn towards me again.

ACT OF LOVE

The lover, the lover will always remember—
That dark man grown hideous with age—
His rough hands upon her white thighs, and the vessel
Gleaming with liquids, ready for his rage,

Holding this moment out of his whole past,
The indecisive dream of wonder, romance:
He will see her as an angel, the nicest
Person in the world, and himself as once

He was, handsome, young. He will always
Remember how she took him to her bed
And performed there under his burning hands,
Until in a cool sleep they lay like dead.

And she too will remember this great love.
It will be bright in her mind. She will live
In the thought of it, and the real present
Will indeed be most hard to forgive.

151

And he, too, has been betrayed,
Will see her lover poised forever over her,
Held in that lusty pose. And he will stop,
As his hand moves like a wind in her deep hair,

To contemplate this infidelity,
How upon his marriage-bed in joy they lay.
And forgiveness, which is so easy, will mean nothing
To one who cannot forget that perfidy.

THE PHALLIC SYMBOL

I saw my scattered hopes upon the floor,
And with them played a horned girl. She was true
To that sculpturesque definition. She was blue
In a bright dress, blue with blue bows.

Behind her stood a man beside the door
To which my eyes rose as he entered, false
With relief I did not feel, certain
It could not be myself, though who else

Could ever have found the room or known
The scene? It was as though a shadow
Of my old self stood indolent by the door,
His face hidden in the grey veil of evening

Which, a shadow itself, encroached across the floor.
Then all the toys cowered in childish terror
In the corner of the room, and the girl became
A little goat, with a beard grey as the river,

Standing uncertain in such a curious meadow
Of dusty floor and cowering toys: and dread
Passed like a shadow across the waiting room.
The man turned from the door and went away:

I saw him retreating down an avenue,
Sinister, unequivocal. And I knew
When I looked at the room again the girl would be
Blue, with the blue dress, and the bow blue

In her beautiful bronze hair: that she would stand
Like a statue, cold and pure, her lips shaped
To a smile: that she would be kind and womanly,
The very definition of what I hoped

To find. And I saw the shadow had filled
The room, and in the darkness I saw nothing.
I heard the dry pad of an animal's feet in the hall,
And then I knew I had no hope at all.

O ROSE, O RAINBOW

Watching the night contract the viridian fields
Into the closeness of its hands, the moon
Athwart the dewy grass, Mr. Orlimpit
Raises his hands towards the glossy dawn,
        Imagining daybreak.

"O Rose, O Rainbow, O hymn of truth, O dew,
Wet my hands, bring me wonder, bring me You,
O great Venus, O doll, o ventriloquist,
Thy sweet rainbow-coloured hands in the evening mist,
        Bringing me rapture..."

153

The exact cadence of his prayer is difficult
To capture; nor do the fields, closed
In the hands of night, feel anything but dark
As towards the dawn his vain hymns are composed,
     Vainly imploring

That dry-eyed goddess. Time in itself is robbed
By the dewy dark of the fields, and the houses stand
Like scaffolds thrown in the shadows
Of the frigid moon. Who can expect to demand
     The rose or the rainbow?

Mr. Orlimpit wanders among his scaffolds,
Erect in the bleak night, false as is dark,
Hoping always for a new star to break, hearing
Only the vain lovers chittering in the park,
     Hoping for heaven.

"I am a fool," says Mr. Orlimpit, "to hope
For anything beyond death. Death is surely
Peace enough. I shall die some day." And then
Mr. Orlimpit imagines his daybreak, its limpid, purely
     Crystalline virtue.

ALCESTIS IN ELY

(*for Priscilla*)

Entering casually the precincts of the Cathedral,
Those old walls, the courtyard with the chestnuts,
Alcestis moves, unmindful of Admetos,
     The modern woman.

Yet her face is pale under the crumbling arches,
As she touches the unnatural red of her lips
With gentle fingers and like a ghost wanders
      Over the cobbles.

And there is no-one to bring her back from death
Nor to remind her of that unmindful king:
Alcestis is alone and cold in Ely
      Among the ancient

Glories of a newer religion. As she takes
Her coffee in Ye Olde Teashoppe she cries
In exasperation, "Where are that man's strong arms?"
      In this town of whispers.

And on its old stones the great Cathedral rises
Like an enormous beast, shaking loose stones
From its side; and the wind blows in the chestnuts,
      Gently discerning.

THE LITTLE GIRL

Yes, true, children will take advantage of
Any little gesture: yet here I saw
More than the villainous eye, the loving
Yet loathing, irrepressible dilemna.

The little girl was old enough to be
My lover, yet she faltered, and I knew
That to my hand her breast would make reply
Hazardously, and probably not true

With responses curious and defined
By some irreparable hoydenish glamour.
O I tried hard to reach her mind,
Yet in her eye there was no glimmer;

Only her legs stretched long upon the sheet
And the big, grown-up, cold-looking feet.

INCIDENTS IN PLAYFAIR HOUSE

I

There are questions that must be asked
That will not—we think— be answered.

Fury is hand in glove with fate: the lion
Is solemn behind the door, the weeping forest

Claims us with its juices, its citrons and pears.
We are all alike unemployed soldiers.

And then —at a distance—a girl stands,
Hands upon her breasts, expectant, fond,

As if waiting for the dark future to come
And wink at her with the eyes of a clown.

We see her. But do not believe. Deceive
Yourself, sir, with many speculations!

Go, drown your horror with philosophy!
Yet what are these questions but the truth that we deserve?

II

O there are monstrous storms! Even the evil—
If we are to believe in such, originally—

Protest at the greatest evils, devils
That irk even the illiterate heart. Start

Praying now, fathomless mouths! The green
Boy is in the field watching the cows

And the prancing horses. The dance,
The horse-dance, the cow-dance, the love-dance

Advances to its climax. Perfection—
Through all storm—gleams like a sheet.

III

Janet, the girl with the bow-tie, the male
Of her family, innately female,

Pisses into the bath-tub. It is her shrubbery.
When she was five—it is our custom

To probe the past to find the present—
She played with little Antony's penis,

And envied it. And this all ended
In a bow-tie. What a comical history!

And now the rush of her water in the bath-tub
Causes the erect Colonel listening in his study

The greatest excitement of his life, the Colonel
Who has murdered Zulus and shot fifteen bears.

Janet is a queer girl, but very handsome:
Much sought after, she is beautiful, but cold.

IV

There is much to be sought. The two plain girls,
One of whom dresses like a man,

Love to be violent as men, to
Talk of art and literature. They like

The male about them. O attractively
The words lisp. The hero grins

In the doorway like a monkey, while they,
Oblivious to the watching eye, make passes,

Body to body, breast to breast, and lie
In a purely literary agony.

O how the oval suns revolve
Blindingly behind each lover's eye!

Douglas Newton

GAIETY OF DESCENDANTS

A Sailor's Song

My calm and herculean dad
Had muscles and the rarest knack
To shrug the muscles that he had

Along his back into a mask:
Mask of a lion's white grimace.

But ah! Alas!
It scared my mother from his bed,
So *he's* alone and *she's* alone:

But I will wear a nightingale
Tattooed upon my shoulder to
Entice my friends into my arms;
Or if my heart's intentions fail
To fly me to the Scilly Islands,
Isles of Scilly, Scilly.

INVASION WEATHER

Two August voices

The summer flows in golden waves
To wash the trees and clean away
A winter's umber from the leaves

And leave them light as glazer's green.
The valley lakes of gold divide
Before the binders' even pace,

Ebb and abide in lively pools,
Until the labourers come
To labour home the wheaty foam.

Harvest! Harvest! the farmers all
—*The Fathers roll their eyeballs underground*—
All the young fork-bearing Neptunes—ah!

But now the avid Fathers sit them down
Upon the fresh raw wracks to supervise
The madmen coupled to the squealing swine:

Yet *still* the lovers lie between the sheaves
—*Though an enormous head glares through the soil*—
Still thigh is whispering to thigh,

And the gold breast rolls on the bronze chest,
An orange softly rolled upon a table;
The little drummer, even's, allowed his dance;

So summer flows. *While under Mycenae*
The ghost of Agamemnon, like a bee,
Hums in the groining of his vaulted tomb.

Norman Nicholson

THE BURNING BUSH

When Moses, musing in the desert, found
The thorn bush spiking up from the hot ground,
And saw the branches on a sudden bear
The crackling yellow barberries of fire,

He searched his learning and imagination
For any logical, neat explanation,
And turned to go, but turned again and stayed
And faced the fire and knew it for his God.

I too have seen the briar alight like coal,
The love that burns, the flesh that's ever whole,
And many times have turned and left it there,
Saying: "It's prophecy—but metaphor."

But stinging tongues like John the Baptist shout:
"That this is metaphor is no way out.
It's dogma too, or you make God a liar;
The bush is still a bush, and fire is fire."

NOW IN THE TIME OF THIS MORTAL LIFE

Frost is tight upon the land
Constricts it with a bony hand,
Yet with blade sharp as a nail
The immanent crocus drills the soil.
Man's nerves aver his spinal wish
And feel the Word becoming Flesh.

God watches soil and spirit mated,
And consecrates what he created,
By raising manhood unto God,
By raising raisins unto blood;
The sacramental prongs reach down
And lift earth to the skies again.
Incarnate God shines brighter than
Flower or frost, or sea or sun.
The Spirit in the limbs of man
Hardens like a skeleton,
And the earth feels a new life burrow
Along its stony bones like marrow.
For now the ritual seed is sown
To grow the stalk to bear the grain
To yield the flour to make the bread
That sinful hands shall turn to God.

The hooks of love are in our limbs
And hoist through the scholastic times
When bursting bud and bomb deny
The Manichaean heresy.
And man finds voice to curse once more
The evil in the holy fear,
And man finds heart to praise again
The hope within the evil pain,
Christ-knife heals the wound it prunes,
And carves its gospel on the bones,
That man may hear what God has heard,
And feel the Flesh becoming Word.

FOR THE NEW YEAR

The stars wheel past the windows
Like flocks of winter sparrows;
The bell clangs out the hours,
And frost sparkles like stars,
And the wind blows up the dawn
With spring behind it and rain
And the spikes of daffodils
And June on fire in the hills.
The apples crowd the bough
Beneath the frosty Plough,
And autumn snow is blown
White as a harvest moon
On currant and raspberry cane,
And the wild ganders fly
Nightly across the sky.
The seasons flit like linnets,
And years whirl past like planets,

And the earth's orbit mars
The changeless map of stars.
The splintered light which now
Gently probes my eye
Is of a star that burned
When the Scots fired the land,
When the Norsemen robbed the dales
And hacked their names on the fells,
Or when the iceberg lakes
Elbowed among the rocks
And carried the Devil's stone
To the hill above the town,
Where through my dormer bay
Drizzles the Milky Way.

COCKLEY MOOR, DOCKRAY, PENRITH

Outside, the cubist fells are drawn again
Beneath the light that speaks ex tempore;
The fur of bracken thickens in the rain
And wrinkles shift upon the scurfy scree.

Inside, like tiles the poet's pleasures lie,
Squares laid on circle, circle laid on square,
And pencilled angles of eternity
Are calculated on the doubled stair.

Outside, the curlew gargles through the mist,
The mountain pansies shut up shop and fade,
The wheatear chisels with his crystal fist,
And day on day like stone on stone is laid.

Inside, are cows on canvas, painted bloom
Fresh as a girl's thin fingers burst to flower,
Bright leaves that do not fall, but fence the room
With the arrested growth of a June hour.

The curving cloud embellishes the sky,
The geometric rain slants to the corn;
Inside, a man remembers he must die,
Outside, a stone forgets that it was born.

THE PREACHERS

The Lord God smiled
  At the mild words
As He heard St. Francis
  Preach to the birds.

Preach of a tree
  With berries on,
That a woman ate
  And gave to a man;

The juice was sweet
  But tart the core,
No herb in field
  Their gripes could cure;

But another tree
  Grew redder fruit,
And there God grafted
  The antidote.

Sparrow and starling,
  Jackdaw and rook
Perched on slates
  And chimney stack.

Tits trapezed
  Upon the spouts,
Starlings dropped lime
  Like marguerites.

They sang to the saint
  With scornful beak:
"The berries give us
  No bellyache.

"But the pips split
  And sprout in man,
And through the thigh
  The roots grow down."

The Lord God laughed
  At the wild fancies
As He heard the birds
  Preach to St. Francis.

CLEATOR MOOR

From one shaft at Cleator Moor
They mined for coal and iron ore.
This harvest below ground could show
Black and red currants on one tree.

In furnaces they burnt the coal,
The ore was smelted into steel,
And railway lines from end to end
Corseted the bulging land.

Pylons sprouted on the fells,
Stakes were driven in like nails,
And the ploughed fields of Devonshire
Were sliced with the steel of Cleator Moor.

The land waxed fat and greedy too,
It would not share the fruits it grew,
And coal and ore, as sloe and plum,
Lay black and red for jamming time.

The pylons rusted on the fells,
The gutters leaked beside the walls,
And women searched the ebb-tide tracks
For knobs of coal or broken sticks.

But now the pits are wick with men,
Digging like dogs dig for a bone:
For food and life we dig the earth—
In Cleator Moor they dig for death.

Every waggon of cold coal
Is fire to drive a turbine wheel;
Every knuckle of soft ore
A bullet in a soldier's ear.

The miner at the rockface stands,
With his segged and bleeding hands
Heaps on his head the fiery coal,
And feels the iron in his soul.

CAROL

Mary laid her Child among
  The bracken-fronds of night—
And by the glimmer round His head
  All the barn was lit.

Mary held her Child above
  The miry, frozen farm—
And by the fire within His limbs
  The resting roots were warm.

Mary hid her Child between
  Hillocks of hard sand—
By singing water in His veins
  Grass sprang from the ground.

Mary nursed her Child beside
  The gardens of a grave—
And by the death within His bones
  The dead became alive.

F. T. Prince

AT A PARADE

We watch the only eagles in the world,
How under the crimson flags they have unfurled
They ruffle in furs and plumes, a rod
Bear or a brazen bonnet nod,
And at their side
Under embroidered sashes long swords, ride

Horses dancing under arms
And bosom-friends to their alarms:
Till with those bugles blowing
The space before the wetly-glowing
Low-lying palace filled up with that crowd,
Your heart and my heart seem to cry aloud.

And standing together and watching, you and I
Have thrown our hearts like caps into the sky.
For as I serve you, so I find
And martialize
Luxurious lucid mind and eyes
To celebrate the moving world.
And though a madness is unfurled,
Though rage and greed would be at blows
And Europe's noisier than a bawdy-house,
What else can I be good for but to praise
And to defend the world, even in these days?

And the soldier is also only a kind of tool
And may be dissolute, foul-mouthed or a fool,
Yet by that animal expense
Bodily brilliance, insolence
It seems that he
May gain peculiar humility.
Therefore we too must be bold
And say these gild the field they hold
Though serving anything
Commended by a criminal century or king
They cover their breasts and shoulders with bright rills
Of glory. It lies in pools about the horses' heels.

Each is the incorruptible masculine
And each remains, though dipped in blood and sin
The lion coloured like a lady
And riding out at dawn is ready
And understands
Why all rewards are wrung out of his hands
Why he dies and knows alone
The order of what was to be done:
I therefore seize those manners,
And moving with that music under banners
I have preserved the pieties that were used
And all the gilded tissues lost, unloosed.

Kathleen Raine

THE CRYSTAL SKULL

I

At the focus of thought there is no face,
the focus of the sun is in crystal with no shadow.
Death of the victim is the power of the god.

Out of the eyes is the focus of love,
the face of love is the sun, that all see,
the skull of the victim is the temple of sight.

The eyes of the victim are the crystal of divination.
Sun clears the colours of life.
The crystal of the skull is the work of the sun.

169

The stone of my destruction casts no shadow.
The sun kills perfectly with the stroke of noon.
The clarity of the crystal is the atonement of the god.

The perfection of man is the pride of death,
the crystal skull is the perpetuity of life.
The power of the god is the taking of love.

The perfection of light is the destruction of the world,
death and love turn the faces of day and night.
The illumination of the skull is the joy of the god.

II

All that will be remembered
  Is a fire
  Rising up to God.
The snow on my love's shoulders
  Will melt in air
  Like a rose fading into night
All that will remain
  Is the fire
  That kindled the heart.

Our lips were the sun setting on snow,
  A cloud
  By day and fire by night.
(All that will be remembered
  Is snow
  Falling on a star)
Now suns are like desire,
  And snow like death
  And eyes the source of light—

But all that will be remembered
Is love
Kindling the night.

Love was in the beginning—the desire
That made a star,
Made man.
All that will remain
Is desire
Returning to God,
All that will be remembered
Is that the sun
Became the heart.

All that will remain
Is man
Consumed by the sun,
All that will remain
Is what the heart remembers
Of the sun.
All that will remain
Is the love
That burns away the sun.

(July 19th, 1941)

"TU NON SE' IN TERRA, SI COME TU CREDI..."

Not upon earth, as you suppose
tower these rocks that turn the wind,
for on their summits angels stand.

Nor from the earth these waters rise—
to quench not thirst, but ecstasy
the waterfall leaps from the sky.

Those nameless clouds that storm and swirl
about the mountain are the veil
that from these sightless eyes shall fall

when senses faint into the ground,
and time and place go down the wind.

ENVOI

Take of me what is not my own,
my love, my beauty, and my poem—
the pain is mine, and mine alone.

See how against the weight in the bone
the hawk hangs perfect in mid-air—
the blood pays dear to raise it there,
the moment, not the bird, divine.

And see the peaceful trees extend
their myriad leaves in leisured dance—
they bear the weight of sky and cloud
upon the fountain of their veins.

In rose with petals soft as air
I bind for you the tides and fire—
the death that lives within the flower,
oh gladly, love, for you I bear!

STILL LIFE

The hour of sight
Flower of light
And unendurable
Wings of flight

All turn to fossil
Turn to stone
The delicate shell
And the mighty bone.

The blood the nerves
The trace of thought
That cross the night
From the source of the world.

The play of light
In the wake of the sun
Is suddenly still
Like a frozen stream

Suddenly still
Bird, flower and shell
That love has created,
Life-shaped and perfected,
So to remain.

LOVE POEM

Yours is the face that the earth turns to me.
Continuous beyond its human features lie
The mountain forms that rest against the sky.

With your eyes, the reflecting rainbow, the sun's light
Sees me; forest and flowers, bird and beast
Know and hold me for ever in the world's thought,
Creation's deep untroubled retrospect.

When your hand touches mine, it is the earth
That takes me—the deep grass,
And rocks and rivers; the green graves,
And children still unborn, and ancestors,
In love passed down from hand to hand from God.
Your love comes from the creation of the world,
From those paternal fingers, streaming through the clouds
That break with light the surface of the sea.

Here, where I trace your body with my hand,
Loves' presence has no end;
For these, your arms that hold me, are the world's.
In us, the continents, clouds and oceans meet
Our arbitrary selves, extensive with the night,
Lost, in the heart's worship, and the body's sleep.

LONDON NIGHT

The sky above London
Last night over my house shone with two kinds of being
And poised between the external and the symbol
I saw Christ's imagined resurrection
Arrayed behind the real September moonlight.

My heart loved and was still,
And to the verge of Heaven so near I stood
That all my lifetime was made less than a moment
For no such Now comes ever with the years' flight.

Not in the grave where we laid our love shall we find him;
The adored one for whom the moonlight was a shroud
Has laid aside the raiment of clouds on the roofs of the houses
Elsewhere and far He died, but here, oh at heart, He rises!

(September 22nd, 1945)

ON LEAVING ULLSWATER

I

The air is full of a farewell—
deserted by the silver lake
lies the wild world, overturned.
Cities rise where mountains fell,
the furnace where the phoenix burned.

II

The lake is in my dream,
the tree is in my blood,
the past is in my bones,
the flowers of the wood
I love with long past loves.
I fear with many deaths
the presence of the night,
and in my memory read
the scripture of the leaves—
      Only myself how strange
      to the strange present come!

NIGHT IN MARTINDALE

Not in the rustle of water, the air's noise,
the roar of storm, the ominous birds, the cries—
the angel here speaks with a human note.

Stone into man must grow, the human word
carved by our whispers in the passing air

is the authentic utterance of cloud,
the speech of flowing water, blowing wind,
of silver moon and stunted juniper.

Words say, waters flow,
rocks weather, ferns wither, winds blow, times go,
I write the sun's Love, and the stars' No.

IN TIME

The beautiful rain falls, the unheeded angel
lies in the street, spreadeagled under the footfall
that from the divine face wears away the smile

whose tears run in the gutter, melting where
the stationary cars wait for departure;
the letter that says Ave is passed over

for at the ever-present place the angel waits,
passes through walls and hoardings, in dark porches
his face, wounded by us, for us and over us watches.

FOR POSTERITY

(On a drawing of Patterdale in 1830)

All life, tumbled together in a storm
And the crags stand out clear in the lightning.
The wind, like a bolting horse, pounds down the valley,
The sheep, like vegetation, draw to earth,
And trees, like animate things, tear at their roots and groan.

That was in 1830. That storm long since was over.
So, my tempestuous love, closed in a quiet book,
And in a quiet grave, disturbs no heart but yours,
Reader, stretched on the summer grass
Waiting for tea-time, and shadows growing longer.

1943.

REQUIEM

Past love, past sorrow, lies this darkness
Where, your face hidden for ever, you are at heart,
Lost from the world yet known to this blind prayer.

Light that divides
Sun from leaf,
Leaf from water,
Water from shadow,
Stone from eye,
Eye from mountain,
The lover from the rose,
Divided us.

Day made us apart,
Lent scope to hate,
To desire, distances,
To despair, perspectives,
To fancies, colour,
To thought, a maze,
To art, semblances.
Light breaks the heart
And shatters love.

But in this dark
Over all dark
Interior dark,
The house of the heart,
Darkness of God,
Blindness of love
Whose eyes have seen
In the sun a cloud
On the perfect face

There is a place
Where living and dead
In love are one.
Your sleep is in my heart,
My dark your rest,
My prayer your peace,
Your death my passion.

April 4th, 1945.

Henry Reed

MORNING

Look, my love, on the wall, and here, at this Eastern picture.
How still its scene, and neither of sleep nor waking:
No shadow falls from the tree or the golden mountain,
The boats on the glassy lake have no reflection,
No echo would come if you blew a horn in those valleys.

And look away, and move. Or speak, or sing:
And voices of the past murmur among your words,
Under your glance my dead selves quicken and stir,
And a thousand shadows attend you where you go.

That is your movement. There is a golden stillness,
Soundless and fathomless, and far beyond it;
When brow on brow, or mouth to mouth assembled,
We lie in the calm of morning. And there, outside us,
The sun moves on, the boat jogs on the lake,
The huntsman calls.
And we lie here, our orient peace awaking,
No echo, and no shadow, and no reflection.

THE DOOR AND THE WINDOW

My love, you are timely come, let me lie by your heart.
For waking in the dark this morning, I woke to that mystery,
Which we can all wake to, at some dark time or another:
Waking to find the room not as I thought it was,
But the window further away, and the door in another di-
    rection.

This was not home, and you were far away
And I woke sick, and held by another passion,
In the icy grip of a dead, tormenting flame,
Consumed by the night, watched by the door and the
  window.
On a bed of stone, waiting for the day to bring you.

The door has opened: and can you, at last beside me,
Drive under the day that frozen and faithless darkness,
With its unseen torments flickering, which neither
The dearest look nor the longest kiss assuages?

Keidrych Rhys

THE GOOD SHEPHERD

(translated from his own Welsh)

Go and spy on the sheep
My father would say
Before I went to school every morning

Today snow covers the ground
On field the sun shone
And the fat sheep cut the trodden patches

I counted them
I looked at their tails!
I found one new lamb and put him to suck

In the zig-zag shelter
Of the hedge by the crooked cart-road.

I smoked a cigarette
That the hired man gave me
There was a lovely slide across the river

I scared the sheep
I bulged after
Through the gap to Old David's cow pasture

Teacher said I never polish my shoes.

THIRD AND FOURTH

When stone-hewn storms knock against our cottage,
What shall we do, my love, my love.
Prove the aspirations of the fourth generation?

Soft buckets from the ivied coalhouse
Out of a too-dear two hundred weights ration
Sitting dusty in seven-day cindery contemplation.

Sprawl on peasant divans on the gingham-checked cushions
    darling

It's war. How shall I feed my unborn baby
Now I'm unemployed and have no money?
Breast feed him?—we're a civilized country.

Lord be good raise a fire in both rooms
Light up the books and rugs the pots and pans
But what if the rain-drops seep in at windowsill
And the wallpaper is damp and dripping?

Is it our nine-days Wind-baby howling outside the house-
    walls?
Now when the garden is old-audacious with snows

Must we put up black-outs against heaven's carpentry?
Prove the aspirations of the fourth generation?

What shall we do, what shall we do?

The retired tavern-keeper is seated alongside our primitive
    villagers under idiot oak-beams
Dismisses the tainted ravings of our poacher-hating farmer
With the double-barrelled B. S. A. shotgun
But should poets half-use binoculars?

Shall I phone for the country G. P., have first-aid ready.
The hot water boiling, a towel. Everything sanitary.
Say: I fear a miscarriage: not diet, worry.

Out of the window, a stack, the cowshed, the smithy.
Ssh! Are you quite happy?
You miss me when I go out of the room.

Announcers and Messerschmitts exhale over our Welsh
    earthsmells
Can't bale out in an Irving: Haw-Haw poisoning the wells.

Dusk's hushed figures slink in the doorways of darkness
They're carrying jugs of water, they're breathless
The pink limed cottages cluster mysterious
Around the four-cornered tower's stillness.

Cast down by hollow suffering I recall
Children in the shade of the Old Chapel wall
The schoolmaster buying a packet of fags at "the Shop"
Kisses on nape of neck pass for a test of heart

In a time of cynicism and rum
So many, so many are longing for husbands to come
Up and squeeze them to their hearts

But here your dear warm afternoon body remains
Proud against pillowslips cross-colour pains
Three wardrobe gargoyles stare at where
Two golden-winged cupids look down from above in their
  rare profusion of hair

Look down upon what cut our bed of love
My love my love what is to be done

O darling shall we curse the Hand above
The Hound of Heaven, the bitchy Joy master,
And the cheap carved bum-dimpled Bacchus, be tried
By all the fertile nightmares of felicity which cried and lied:
Be interrupted in the flame of midnight by demands—
Imagination hearkening along bumpy catcall lands
. . . And once for months, Oh absent months with tears
Quick tears, I sickened for your off-blue whiteness!
No. Step out of shoulder-straps marriage resurrects holiness?
Who saddens us now with bellowing . . . ties also the
  clovergift?

Does the storm abate its puffed-cheek breath, then start again?
Who says:
There is a spot moving somewhere in air?

Is there no-one no-one no-one to prove, prove aspiration
Prove the aspirations of the fourth generation

I ponder too long the X-ray child in his mother's womb.

Anne Ridler

A DREAM OBSERVED

Out from his bed the breaking seas
  By waking eyes unseen
Now fall, aquatic creatures whirl
  And he whirls through the ambient green.

The sea lion and the scolopendra
  Lolling in sleep he sees
Strange in their ways, and the swift changes
  Their landscape makes, from shells to trees.

Down English lanes a camel walks,
  Or untrammelled flies.
But I, wakeful and watching, see
  How chilly out of the clothes he lies.

Easy an act to cover him warm:
  Such a lover's small success
Like the heaped mind so humble in sleep
  But points our actual powerlessness.

Monsters in dreams he sees, yet lies
  At peace in his curling bed;
Blessings that outdo all distress
  Implicit in his sleeping head.

BEFORE SLEEP

Now that you lie
  In London afar,
And may sleep longer
  Though lonelier,
For I shall not wake you
  With a nightmare,
Heaven plant such peace in us
As if no parting stretched between us.

The world revolves
  And is evil;
God's image is
  Wormeaten by the devil;
May the good angel
  Have no rival
By our beds, and we lie curled
At the sound unmoving centre of the world.

In our good nights
  When we were together,
We made, in that stillness
  Where we loved each other,
A new being, of both
  Yet above either:
So, when I cannot share your sleep,
Into this being, half yours, I creep.

FOR A CHILD EXPECTED

Lovers whose lifted hands are candles in winter,
Whose gentle ways like streams in the easy summer,
Lying together

185

For secret setting of a child, love what they do,
Thinking they make that candle immortal, those streams
  forever flow,
And yet do better than they know.

So the first flutter of a baby felt in the womb,
Its little signal and promise of riches to come,
Is taken in its father's name;
Its life is the body of his love, like his caress,
First delicate and strange, that daily use
Makes dearer and priceless.

Our baby was to be the living sign of our joy,
Restore to each the other's lost infancy;
To a painter's pillaging eye
Poet's coiled hearing, add the heart we might earn
By the help of love; all that our passion would yield
We put to planning our child.

The world flowed in; whatever we liked we took:
For its hair, the gold curls of the November oak
We saw on our walk;
Snowberries that make a Milky Way in the wood
For its tender hands; calm screen of the frozen flood
For our care of its childhood.

But the birth of a child is an uncontrollable glory;
Cat's cradle of hopes will hold no living baby,
Long though it lay quietly.
And when our baby stirs and struggles to be born
It compels humility: what we began
Is now its own.

For *as the sun that shines through glass*
So Jesus in His Mother was.
Therefore every human creature,
Since it shares in His nature,
In candle gold passion or white
Sharp star should show its own way of light.
May no parental dread or dream
Darken our darling's early beam:
May she grow to her right powers
Unperturbed by passion of ours.

BUNHILL'S FIELDS

Under cool trees the City tombs
    extend, and nearer lie
stones above Blake's and Bunyan's bones
    to Vivian's working days than I.

Since he is gentle, wild and good
    as you were, peaceable Shades,
there may he' go within your care
    as in my heart his love resides.

Such a care as held unharmed
    the tree within the fire;
spread wings like those that led
    Tobias in the dangerous shire.

And if I fear his death too much,
    let me not learn more faith
by sad trial of what I dread,
    nor grieve him by my own death.

For our faith is one which may
   convert but not console:
we shall not, except by our own will,
   part for ever in the gape of hell.

EDLESBOROUGH

Beyond the Chiltern coast, this church:
A lighthouse in dry seas of standing corn.
Bees hive in the tower; the outer stone
Pared and frittered in sunlight, flakes with the years:
Clunch crumbles, but silence, exaltation, endures.

The brass-robed Rector stretched on his tomb endures.
Within, we go upon the dragon and the bat,
Walk above the world, without,
Uplifted among grey lavender, beech and sycamore,
Shades of the sea-born chalk, indelible and austere.

If we see history from this hill
It is upon its own conditions, here
Each season swirls and eddies the circle of a year
Round the spectator church, and human eyes
Take, on its plinth, a long focus of centuries.

We seem like gods on any hill.
From here all toil resembles rest, and yet
Unlike a god we feel ourselves shut out.
Surely that farm in a carved blue curve of trees
So still with all its creatures, holds the unattainable peace

It is Time's camouflage deceives us.
There it extends like space: whatever moves

(A horse to drink, a reaper to stack the sheaves)
Displays the movement in its whole succession,
Not a change of terms, only a changed relation.

Deceit or truth? The dead possess the hill
In battlements of Totternhoe or slate;
The view is ours, the range and ache of sight.
If Time serves: in a common space unrolls
This Resurrection field, with sheaves in glory like risen souls.

POEM FOR A CHRISTMAS BROADCAST

Woman's Voice

Perhaps you find the angel most improbable?
It spoke to men asleep, their minds ajar
For once to admit the entrance of a stranger.
Few have heard voices, but all have made a journey:
The mind moves, desiring dedication,
Desiring to lay its gifts, as a dog its bone,
At the feet of the first creation. "Take it or leave it"
Says pride, "You made it; You must bear the blame."
But secretly the heart — "O make it good."
"Either God acts in vain, or this is God."

1st King

Melchior brings gold. O teach me to give,
For this was infancy's first love:
Its first possession; its adult passion—
O new creation
Take my treasure and make me free.

2nd King

Caspar, incense: all that is strange,
Oblique, projected beyond the range
Of the First Person. Such mediation
O new creation
Take, that we dare the direct sight.

3rd King

Death is a strong wish. Balthasar
Brings his desire in a gift of myrrh;
Seeking perfection in pain and cessation—
O new creation
Die for me, make me desire to live.

All Three

Mary, who nourished glory on human kindness
By springs of power hidden from the mind,
Here is our small self-knowledge, now
Make it acceptable, or teach us how.

Mary

He will accept it, never fear,
For his audacity is my despair.
O do not give what he should not bear.
His boldness is beyond belief,
His threats, his lightnings, his short grief.
Is it divine or mortal confidence?
Mortal ignorance, godlike innocence.
Brazen, he takes love as a right;

He knows to demand is to give delight.
Youngling, here we offer love—
What have we to offer but love?—
And what is our love? Greed and despair.
O do not take what you should not bear,
Or tainted love by true convince:
Let us not harm you, helpless Prince.
Sin is the chance of mercy;
Then even sin contrives your greater glory.

THE SPRING EQUINOX

Now is the pause between asleep and awake:
Two seasons take
A colour and quality each from each as yet.
The new stage-set—
Spandril, column and fan—of spring is raised against the
  winter backdrop
Murrey and soft;
Now aloft
The sun swings on the equinoctial line.
Few flowers yet shine:
The hellebore hangs a clear green bell and opulent leaves
  above dark mould;
The light is cold
In arum leaves, and a primrose flickers
Here and there; the first cool bird-song flickers in the thicket.
Clouds are pale as the pollen from sallows;
March fallows are white with lime like frost.

This is the pause between asleep and awake:
The pause of contemplation and of peace,

Before the earth must teem and the heart ache.
This is the child's pause, before it sees
That the choice of one way has denied the other;
Must choose the either, or both, of to care and not to care;
Before the light or darkness shall discover
Irreparable loss; before it must take
Blame for the creature caught in the necessary snare:
Receiving a profit, before it holds a snare.

Lynette Roberts

POEM FROM LLANYBRI

If you come my way that is...
Between now and then, I will offer you
A fist full of rock cress fresh from the bank
The valley tips of garlic red with dew
Cooler than shallots, a breath you can swank

In the village when you come. At noon-day
I will offer you a choice bowl of cawl
Served with a "lover's" spoon and a chopped spray
Of leeks or savori fach, not used now,

In the old way you'll understand. The din
Of children singing through the eyelet sheds
Ringing 'smith hoops, chasing the butt of hens;
Or I can offer you Cwmcelyn spread

With quartz stones from the wild scratchings of men:
You will have to go carefully with clogs
Or thick shoes for it's treacherous the fen,
The East and West Marshes also have bogs.

Then I'll do the lights, fill the lamp with oil,
Get coal from the shed, water from the well;
Pluck and draw pigeon with crop of green foil
This your good supper from the lime-tree fell.

A sit by the hearth with blue flames rising,
No talk. Just a stare at "Time" gathering
Healed thoughts, pool insight, like swan sailing
Peace and sound around the home, offering

You a night's rest and my day's energy.
You must come—start this pilgrimage
Can you come? send an ode or elegy
In the old way and raise our heritage.

THE SHADOW REMAINS

To speak of everyday things with ease
And arrest the mind to a simpler world
Where living tables are stripped of a cloth;

Of wood on which I washed, sat at peace:
Cooked duck, shot on an evening in peacock cold:
Studied awhile: wrote: baked bread for us both.

But here by the hearth with leisured grace
I prefer to speak of the vulgar clock that drips
With the falling of rain: woodbine tips, and yarrow

Spills, lamp, packet of salt, and twopence of mace
That sit on the shelf edged with a metal strip,
And below, brazier fire that burns our sorrow,

Dries weeping socks above on the rack: that knew
Two angels pinned to the wall—again two.

LOW TIDE

Every waiting moment is a fold of sorrow
Pierced within the heart.
Pieces of mind get torn off emotionally
In large wisps.
Like a waif I lie, stillbound to action:
Each waiting hour I stare and see not,
Hum and hear not, nor care I how long
The lode mood lasts.

My eyes are raw and wide apart
Stiffened by the salt bar
That separates us.
You so far;
I at ease at the hearth
Glowing for a welcome
From your heart.
Each beating moment crosses my dream
So that wise things cannot pass
As we had planned.
Woe for all of us: supporting those
Who like us fail to steel their hearts,
But keep them wound in clocktight rooms,
Ill found. Unused. Obsessed by time.
Each beating hour
Rings false.

W. R. Rodgers

THE SWAN

Bottomed by tugging combs of water
The slow and loath swan slews and looks
Coldly down through chutes of stilled chatter
Upon the shadows in flight among the stones.

Into abashed confusions of ooze
It dips, and from the muddy fume
The filtered and flute like fishes rise
Endlessly up through all their octaves of gloom.

To where the roofed swan suavely swings
Without qualm on the footling wave
That laves it on, with elbowing wings swelled
Wide under its eyes' held look and architrave.

Slow slow it slides, as if not to chafe
The even sleeve of its approach
Stretched stiff and oval in front of it,
Siphoning it on, selfless, silent and safe.

Jonquil-long its neck adjudicates
Its body's course, aloof and cool
It cons the nonchalant face of air
With its incurious and dispassionate stare.

On that grey lake frilled round with scufflings
Of foam, and milled with muttering,

I saw, lingering late and lightless,
A single swan swinging, sleek like a sequin.

Negligently bright, wide wings pinned back,
It mooned on the moving water,
And not all the close and gartering dark
Or levering winds could lift or flatter

That small and dimming image into flight,
Far from shore and free from foresight,
Coiled in its own indifferent mood
It held the heavens, shores, waters and all their brood.

AUTUMN

                Going out, those bold days,
O what a gallery-roar of trees and gale-wash
Of leaves abashed me, what a shudder and shore
Of bladdery shadows dashed on windows ablaze,
What a hedge-shingle seething, what vast lime-splashes
Of light clouting the land. Never had I seen
Such a running-over of clover, such tissue sheets
Of cloud poled asunder by sun, such plunges
And thunder-load of fun. Trees, grasses, wings—all
On a hone of wind sluiced and sleeked one way,
Smooth and close as the pile of a pony's coat,
But, in a moment, smoke-slewed, glared, squinted back
And up like sticking bones shockingly unkinned.
How my heart, like all these, was silk and thistle
By turns, how it fitted and followed the stiff lifts
And easy falls of them, or, like that bird above me,
No longer crushing against cushions of air,

Hung in happy apathy, waiting for wind-rifts.
Who could not dance on, and be dandled by such a day
Of loud expansion? when every flash and shout
Took the hook of the mind and reeled out the eye's line
Into whips and whirl-spools of light, when every ash-shoot
   shone
Like a weal and was gone in the gloom of the wind's lash.
Who could not feel it? the uplift and total substraction
Of breath as, now bellying, now in abeyance,
The gust poured up from the camp's throat below, bringing
Garbled reports of guns and bugle-notes,
But, gullible, then drank them back again.
And I, dryly shuffling through the scurf of leaves
Fleeing like scuffled toast, was host to all these things;
In me were the spoon-swoops of wind, in me too
The rooks dying and settling like tea-leaves over the trees;
And, rumbling on rims of rhyme, mine were the haycarts
   home-creeping
Leaving the rough hedge-cheeks long-strawed and streaked
   with their weeping.

LENT

Mary Magdalene, that easy woman,
Saw, from the shore, the seas
Beat against the hard stone of Lent;
Crying "Weep, seas, weep
For yourselves that cannot dent me more."

"O more than all these, more crabbed than all stones,
And cold, make me, who once
Could leap like water, Lord. Take me

As one who owes now
Nothing to what she was. Ah, naked.

My waves of scent, my petticoats of foam,
Put from me and rebut;
Disown. And that salt lust stave off
That slavered me—O
Let it whiten in grief against the stones

And outer reefs of me. Utterly doff,
Nor leave the lightest veil
Of feeling to heave or soften.
Nothing cares this heart
What hardness crates it now or coffins.

Over the balconies of these curved breasts
I'll no more peep to see
The light procession of my loves
Surf-riding in to me
Who now have eyes and alcove, Lord, for Thee."

"Room, Mary," said He, "ah make room for me
Who am come so cold now
To my tomb." So, on Good Friday,
Under a frosty moon
They carried Him and laid Him in her womb.

A grave and icy mask her heart wore twice,
But on the third day it thawed,
And only a stone's-throw away
Mary saw her God.
—Did you hear me?—Mary saw her God.

Dance, Mary Magdalene, dance, dance and sing,
For unto you is born
This day a King. "Lady," said He,
"To you who relent
I bring back the petticoat and the bottle of scent."

NEITHER HERE NOR THERE

In that land all is, and nothing's Ought;
No owners or notices, only birds;
No walls anywhere, only lean wire of words
Worming brokenly out from eaten thought;
No oats growing, only ankle-lace grass
Easing and not resenting the feet that pass;
No enormous beasts, only names of them;
No bones made, bans laid, or boons expected,
No contracts, entails, hereditaments,
Anything at all that might tie or hem.

In that land all's lackadaisical;
No lakes of coddled spawn, and no locked ponds
Of settled purpose, no netted fishes;
But only inkling streams and running fronds
Fritillaried with dreams, weedy with wishes;
Nor arrogant talk is heard, haggling phrase,
But undertones, and hesitance, and haze;
On clear days mountains of meaning are seen
Humped high on the horizon; no one goes
To con their meaning, no one cares or knows.

In that land all's flat, indifferent; there
Is neither springing house nor hanging tent,
No aims are entertained, and nothing is meant,

For there are no ends and no trends, no roads,
Only follow your nose to anywhere.
No one is born there, no one stays or dies,
For it is a timeless land, it lies
Between the act and the attrition, it
Marks off bound from rebound, make from break, tit
From tat, also to-day from to-morrow.
No Cause there comes to term, but each departs
Elsewhere to whelp its deeds, expel its darts;
There are no homecomings, of course, no good-byes
In that land, neither yearning nor scorning,
Though at night there is the smell of morning.

SONG FOR WAR

Put away the flutes
Into their careful clefts,
And cut the violins that like ivy climb
Flat to their very roots;
All that a subtler time
Allowed us we must now commute
To commoner modes; for here come
The hieratic trumpet and demotic drum
Fall in and follow, let the beat
Hyphenate your halved feet,
Feel its imbricating rhythm
Obliterating every schism
And split through which you might espy
The idiosyncratic I;
Let the assumptive trumpets pace
And pattern out the sounding space
Into stillnesses that numb

By iteration and by sum,
Till the walls of will fall down
Round the seven-times-circled town
Of your mind, and not a jot
Is left of fore or after thought.
O slowly go and closely follow,
Toe to heel and hill to hollow,
All the ditto feet that lead
You onward in a millipede
To the battle where, as one,
A hundred thousand tip and run.

But when the burning sun again
Behind the hill
Slides down and leaves the separate slain
Frosted and still,
Then over the rued fields that drum and trumpet fled
Slow musics rise like mists and wreathe their requiem
Round the bruised reeds, and coldy mounts the moon
Of thought, and rules among the quorum of the dead.

SONG FOR PEACE

See, the ruthless victor comes
With tooth of trumpet, claw of drums,
Have ready on his route
A fanfare of strumpets and a salute
Of fifty bums;
This, this will be his randy-vous
With destiny; have handy, too,
The boostings of applause
To blow his fuses and effect a pause.
And you, you tuneless walls,

201

Open wide the windows of your huff
And hang out every hoarse hurrah,
Brighten your doorways, do your stuff,
And draw him from his coup d'etat;
Bring out the dancing flute
And the frivolous fiddle,
Merry-go-round and inveigle
Him into the middle,
Until his sidelong glances scrape
Across the feminine violin-shape,
And his obedient battalions
Caper on curtseying feet like stallions.

Yet if this fails, fails to move
Him from his humdrummed groove,
And if the hammered round
Of order and routine
Allows no new, no extraordinary sound
To dent, to enter, or to intervene;
If in the fixed receipt
Of war's auricular beat
He marches on unvarying and complete,
Then some disharmony we must devise
Him to divide against himself and civilise:
Then let the still small voice
Connive, contrive
To enter a caveat against
Each move by which he would arrive:
Veto no destination, but instead
Insert a doubt into his very tread;
See that his single track of feeling frays
Into two sudden, different, equal ways;

Between his "I will" and "I ought"
Cause him to halt and stand in thought;
Force him to pick and predicate
Each walking step and waking state;
Till his one-way-street of going
Vacillates into to-and-froing,
And his flowing roundabout
Of.feeling flounders into doubt
And angular analysis
Of self and its paralysis.

At last, at last his listless hand lets fall
The pulseless drum.
And the uncertain trumpet asks
The way to kingdom-come,
And Peace comes forward now, him to inurn.
Ring bells, and bawl hooray,
Empty is war's highway,
And men to subtler routes and set pursuits return.
And yet,
As quavering rings of sound
Surround the clanged gong,
Wrinkling on long after and far out,
In mind we may prolong
Beyond the body's bound
The wavering flounces of that martial shout
That once called all men up and coiled them round
With rhythm that now is fallen utterly into rout.

NATIVITY

His holly hair, his berry eye are here,
And his chrysanthemum wound,

This Christmas day; by symbols once again
The Mystery's importuned.

Hisses the singing kettle of his blood
Out of his sanguine side,
Poked by the sibling spear it ebbs and flows
In a hub-bubble tide

That dyes the silent room. The gay young god,
Dog in the manger now,
Growls in the hearth, and bares old teeth against
The Ass in us, the Cow.

There are the portly bottle-loins, and there
The wine-marks of his birth
Upon the straw, the biscuit-brittle straw
Broken by Mary's girth.

And here, most meek, most eager, and most hushed,
The angelic agents hover,
A great prudential company, all come
To offer him life-cover.

Comes Sentiment with frozen tears lent
By Memory, melting sweet,
Her hothead cries boil over and congeal
Again at her cold feet.

And Grief, deep in her crushed and tinfoil wrap,
Brokenly glares to-day
Among the ashes and the cruel butt-
Ends of this Christmas play.

And there's the tapering tree of his descent,
Hitched toa kingly star,
Earth is its horizontal, heaven and hell
Its upright centre-spar.

The very tree of life, so base, so wide,
And with such longing fraught,
Up the step-ladder of our looks it spires
Into a point of thought.

In the stark winter of our tinselled pride
Its frozen growth now stands
Waiting the fiery gift, the melting dew
Spangled from heavenly hands.

Ah look! The bush is candlabraed now
With yellow and with blue,
Types of the spirit, sweet and bitter both,
Opposed but wholly true.

Outside, like rootless souls the silent trees
Sail past on trays of mist;
The miser-icicle on the pane still marks
The place that Judas kissed.

His thistle breath still lingers in the air,
Spiky with eagerness,
It hovers on the garden, and the grass
Whitens at his caress.

Robin with rusty bib no longer can
Pull out the worm-like nail,

Dumpy with impotence it droops and humps
Upon the wooden rail.

And hark! The Herod-angels sing tonight!
Over the Magi's tents
Their heartless song drones on through grumbling gloom
And weeping continents.

High on his farthing floor the airman moons
Above the mourning town
Of Bethlehem; it is his footling root
And he the flower and crown.

O Caspar, Melchior, and Balthazer,
Come from your caravan
And tell me where you go, and what new star
You saw in Teheran:

And what new man now hurries to be born
Out of our addled earth,
And O what silly corner of ourselves
Will see the mangy birth.

Strike, strike the gong of our song till souls take fire,
Clasp hands and bellow,
Dance, dance, leap higher and longer, and hug
Each with its fellow.

Lord, in this wintry interval we send
Our indolent regards
And grey regrets. Make fluent all the pens
Of all the frozen bards.

Lay the live coal upon their lips that they
May leap uproariously
Out of their huff of words, and let the thorns
Crackle with prophecy.

Resume, and reimburse the silent wood,
Elaborate its saps,
Bid the bare trees blurt into bloom, and fill
With leaf the hungry gaps,
And in its head set the heart's singing birds.

D. S. Savage

WINTER OFFERING

All I can offer now is a cracked china jug
Of water, and, grown with tedious sweat and toil,
Potatoes from the back-garden clods dug,
Cut with the blunt spade-edge, clogged with heavy soil.

I wish I could give you apples, grapes and pears,
I wish I could give you cider and sour wine,
But the orchard has been rank and green for years
And its fruit won't ripen without sunshine.

Potatoes cement bone, keep body and soul together,
Water costs nothing and will do for the present.
It's difficult enough to be gay in this wretched weather
Without useless regrets for living like a peasant.

We'll make no virtue of enforced economy,
Strike no impressive plaster or tin attitudes.

207

Poverty's fixed, archaic physiognomy
Projects only through masks where nothing else extrudes.

THE WILD SWAN

The evening spread its rags of melancholy
over the marshes where the pylons traced
a windy track. The air was desolate
with sorrow unexpressed, and the birds sang
as though their songs were the faint whispers of wind
that broke, sighing, upon the singing reeds.

Wind faltered hesitantly through the viaduct
that spanned the river, and stilled on the cold surface
of stone. My mind was hard and sensitive
as that dark mirror in its loneliness;
but as my glancing eyes met the still waters
the lake was splintered by a lacing swan:
my mood was shattered with its calm explosion.

FEBRUARY

Ebbs from soiled fields the last drab vestige of snow,
Through February's veils the hazy distance looms,
In sunken woods no melancholy horn is blown,
Only an invisible process of decay consumes.

I have sat at this window and watched the day
Consumed as though its substance were a powdering wood
In whose grey embers the origin of all decay
Smouldered, as it patiently smoulders within my blood.

Rotting vegetation, a leaf like a leather glove,
A glove or a fleshless hand, of a corpse or a tree;
Excrement; a dead dog buried in a garden grave;
I am all these, and all these moulder in me.

I am the limestone in the cave, the putrefying bone,
The seashell mashed and splintered by the mechanical surf,
The green, soft fallen tree-trunk, the crumbling stone,
The waterlogged carrion under the thatch of turf.

The odour of mortality rises from the death of the day,
Earth's subtle chemistry proceeds; water drips from the boughs;
Nourished on black corruption, warmed in the breath of decay
The seeds of Spring lie swelling in their soaking house.

SCENARIO

A door creaks in the house. Outside the window
rain streams upon the flat, deserted landscape.
It falls from everlasting to everlasting.
The earth hungers. Trees spread their gaunt limbs wider.

"I had a lover, but because of my soul's depravity
Time soured him like a crust, we were chained like prisoners.
Now he replenishes the earth, his breast is hollow,
he is gone from me like a rotten tooth, leaving an aching cavity.

"I, alone, beneath the groaning rooftree,
agonize in desperation, and in a crazy fashion
I am like a wet fag-end left smouldering
on the edge of a fouled sink, rank with my wry passion."

The wind rattles the windows. In a dirty saucer
mix ash and tea-stains. The woman wanders.
Cinematic memory unwinds the defunct weathers
of a hundred wasted seasons, but supplies no answer.

SEPARATION

All day I have been completely alone, and now the night
Descends, swathing in shadow and swaddling all,
And all but a smother and blur is bandaged from sight,
Blots and blotches of shadow clotting on ceiling and wall.

I lift the glass chimney, and light the oil-lamp's wick,
The quick lick of the flame flickers, and shadows distend,
The elongations of fingers sprawl on the wall, and the tick
Of the tin clock in the silence and the tick of my pulse contend.

In this prolongation of solitude, I am estranged
Even from myself, in you; in your absence I dwindle apart
In a ghostly attenuation of feeling, till all my deranged
Consciousness aches in the void for the physical thud of your
    heart.

LIVING

The smoky blue of evening wreathes from fields
        Of tumbled clay,
And lanes where summer's trampled body sprawls
        In damp decay.

Through the thin mist, a heavy tread encroaching,
        I greet my neighbor

Clumsily slouching homeward to his cottage,
    Tired after labour.

Alone with dusk, I light a cigarette,
    But let it smoulder.
Another year burns down to stub and ash,
    And I am older.

CONFESSION

You have said, for certain
To be true, to be good
Words must be written
In the heart's blood.

I have tried, I have tried,
I have labored and toiled
Till the ink dried
Or the blood cooled.

I know that blood is bitter,
That ink tastes sour,
The hand runs better
When the heart is sure.

I walk among men
With my labour and pain,
Blood on the pen,
Ink in the vein.

ABSENT CREATION

I wait for wonder, or the weather's turn
To teach my tongue to wind its tangled skein
Of loss or love, lilt out its awkward words,
Or learn a rhythm from the weaving rain.

I await that ease and excellence of mind
That intimates suave movement to the hand,
Letting the typewriter shuttle off its lines
To a slow march, or stately saraband.

But time and tide-turn, running past the ear,
Seethe with distraction on a wasting sound,
The hour-sands plunge, my fingers plough through care,
I hear an endless clock thud underground.

Upon this desert coast, this sea examinate,
Lord, burst a cyclone, or a soothing rain,
Detonate dams, flood cities, souse or intoxicate,
That I may live, and feel, and speak again!

Francis Scarfe

TYNE DOCK

The summer season at Tyne Dock
Hoisted my boyhood in a crane
Above the shaggy mining town,
Above the slaghills and the rocks,
Above the middens in backlanes
And wooden hen-huts falling down.

Vermilion grass grew in the street
Where the blind pit-ponies pranced
And poppies screamed by butchers' stalls
Where bulls kicked sparks with dying feet,
And in the naked larks I sensed
A cruel god beneath it all.

Over the pit-head wheel the moon
Was clean as a girl's face in school;
I envied the remote old man
Who lived there, happy and alone,
While in the kitchen the mad spool
Unwound as Annie's treadle ran.

The boyish season is still there
For clapping hands and leaping feet
Across the slagheaps and the dunes;
And still it breaks into my care,
Though I will never find the street,
Nor catch the old, impulsive tune,
Nor ever lose that child's despair.

(April, 1947)

THE GROTTO

The sea still plunges where as naked boys
We dared the currents and the racing tides
That stamped red weals of fury on our thighs,
Yet did not know our first love was the sea
That rolled like colts between our shining knees,
While under us the sands in golden curls
Coiled round our bodies like the plaits of girls.

We came oblique to passion on that shore
Identified with our blind will to danger,
As when we explored the slipping walls of caves
Booming with dark more fearful than the waves
Whose silence magnified the heart's deep roar
Till senses beat that were asleep before,
And in ourselves we recognized a stranger.

Or when we scaled by Frenchman's Bay the cliff
No man has dared—though boys there in the night
Still prove their manhood on its hostile side—
That was our climb from innocence to life;
And yet, if I could be there once again,
My love, I'd pause amazed among the gulls,
Afraid of both the triumphs and the falls.

In sea and grotto where we found our hearts
Our youth remained, and all our days return
In dream and vision to the mocking sea
Where womanhood and manhood proudly stirred
Within our silence like a singing bird,
And never a dawning day will break as pure
As our grave adoration, immature.

THE CLOCK

Far away is one who now is sleeping
In the same world and the same darkness,
  But not in my keeping.
Oh no, my arms could never stretch so far
And my hands trembling with tenderness
  Cannot hope to caress
Her limbs, save by remembering what they are.

214

Oh no, my words must never reach her ears
That lie so white against her sombre hair,
  No, no, she must not hear
My voice that has no happiness to bring,
For she also is lost in a realm where
  My cry and my despair
Are out of tune whatever song they sing.

Perhaps as I lie waking she is dreaming,
But not of me, for dreams are not so kind;
  While my eyes are brimming
With images of things that might have been,
And my lips for a prayer for her peace of mind
  That, early, she may find
A love more delicate and more serene.

And all my body prays her to forget
  One who long cared for her too bitterly,
One who is in her debt
For the clock of suffering that kept, twelve years
The hours of absence and futility,
  Who could love utterly
Beyond the meaning of these words and tears.

CATS

Those who love cats which do not even purr
Or which are thin and tired and very old,
Bend down to them in the street and stroke their fur
And rub their ears, and smooth their breast, and hold
Them carefully, and gaze into their eyes of gold.

For how can they pass what does not ask for love
But draws it out of those who have too much,
Frustrated souls who cannot use it all, who have
Somewhere too tight and sad within them, such
A tenderness it flows through all they touch.

They are the ones who love without reward,
Those on whom eyes are closed, from whom heads turn,
Who know only too well they can afford
To squander love, since in the breast it burns
With the cold anguish every lover learns.

So they pass on, victims of silent things,
And what they love remains indifferent
And stretches in the sun and yawns, or licks the rings
That sheathe its claws, or sleeps and is content,
Not knowing who she was, or what she meant.

THE WINDOW

In after years, when you look back upon
This time, and upon me, who am no more
Close to your heart nor a shadow in your sun,
Perhaps you will stand still and lean on the door
Or lay down something, feeling quite undone.

Some passing stranger, or a turn of phrase,
Or any echo or shade, will be enough,
Anything that is worn and almost effaced,
Anything half finished, will be proof
I was no natural but an acquired taste.

216

So you will stand there, looking back, inspired
As though the curtains parted on some view
Not quite to be believed in, nor desired,
And which did not exist except for you,
Like some clay thing the potter never fired.

No, it would not be wise to throw the window wide.
Close it quickly, before it hurts, and go
About your usual tasks, and let time hide
Beneath mountains of hours, what you know
Cannot be lived again, yet has not died.

PROGRESSION

See that satan pollarding a tree,
That geometric man straightening a road:
Surely such passions are perverse and odd
That violate windows and set the north wind free.

No doubt tomorrow the world will be too straight.
Five hundred miles an hour will churn our dreams
Like surprised whales, when we lie a dead weight
In an ignorant sleep, and things will be what they seem.

Tomorrow we will hear on the gramophone
The music of the Spheres, registered H.M.V.
By a divorced contralto: we shall perhaps
Meet Adam under glass in a museum
Fleshless and most unlovely, complete with pedigree.

Or else, tomorrow, workers, kings and crooks
Will all have aeroplanes and be fast friends,
In a world no longer divided by dividends,
Where love will be almost as simple as it looks.

217

Sidney Goodsir Smith

LARGO

Ae boat anerlie nou
Fishes frae this shore,
Ae black drifter lane
Riggs the crammasie daw,
Aince was a fleet, and nou
Ae boat alane gaes oot.

War ir Peace, the trawlers win
An the youth turns awa
Bricht wi baubles nou
An thirled tae factory ir store;
Their faithers fished their ain,
Unmaistered; —ane remains.

And never the clock rins back,
The free days are owre;
The warld shrinks, we luik
Mair t'oor maisters ilka hour—
Whan yon lane boat I see
Daith an rebellion blinn ma ee!

(anerlie - only; crammasie - crimson; daw - dawn; thirled - thralled)

CAN I FORGET?

Can I forget the sickle mune
Owre Largo throu the driven clouds,
The sea lik bilan milk at oor fit?
Can I forget the snaw aroun

218

An the tent-flap lik a gun boom
Whan the wund tuik it?

Can I forget the wolves' houl
Famished rinnan throu the toun
O' haar an wund an lamplicht?
Can I forget the staucheran news
As Christ received the Spanish doom
An nocht tae dae but drink o nichts?

Can I forget ma black wound?
Kirdcudbright, may ye be dung doun
An dammed, Dundrennan too!
Can I forget, (Och, never!) a luve
Crottle in my twa haunds tae stour,
The rose o ma hert wormed wi rue?

Can I forget the Solway flows
Gray as daith, or the worm i' the rose?
Whiles, whiles; but it bides its hour.
O, thornèd nou, hert's fanatic pouer
Strang as the skaith's a meisure o the luve.

Can I forget whit the saul can prove,
That luve is bricht as the skaith is durc,
The skaith is deep as the luve is hie?
Can I forget I'll neer can lose
Twa tyger een nae mair nor those
Lang houghs lik the silken dunes o the sea?

Can I forget, ma luve, ma luve,
Havana thrang wi drucken fules

219

And ye amang them, lauchan queen?
Can I forget, ma luve, ma luve,
Strathyre's muckle bed in a wee room,
White breists lik hills i the mune's lily leam?

Can I forget the gifts o you,
Yon music that's the wine o luve,
The birds' wild sea-sang in yir hair?
Can I forget, ma pouter doo,
Voar an hairst an winter are you,
Sun an mune an the warld, ma dear?

(fit - feet; haar - sleet; wund - wind; staucherin - staggering; crottle - crumble away; stour - dust; skaith - wound; houghs - thighs; lauchan - laughing; leam - gleam; pouter doo - pouter dove; voar - spring; hairst - autumn)

WHAN THE HERT IS LAICH

Lamb, whan the hert is laich,
Lourd wi' the haill warld's wecht,
A boulder's whare the hert shud be,
A muckle stane that burdens yee.

Ye sit lik a cairn o stane yersel,
The burds' blye sangs ye hear wi laith,
The sakless burn rins doun tae hell,
The aince-luved trees a choir o daith.

An whitna cause ye mayna tell
Nor casting reason bring release,
Ye sit lik a stane an watch the hills
That mock yir thrawan with their peace.

(Laich - low, lourd - heavy, haill - whole, wecht - weight, muckle - great, laith - loathe, loth, blye - blithe, sakless - blameless, burn - brook, whitna - whatever, thrawan - throes)

SANG: RECOLL O SKAITH

Wersh an drumlie are the lees
Ma lips are suppan nou,
Wersh an wan the bitter bree
Bled frae the skaith o luve;
O wald I'd flee the thochts that ding,
Thir nichts I mayna sleep,
But aye the gorgoulls gowl ahint
An roun ma hert they creep.

O wersh the lees that curl ma lips
An sick ma stoundit saul,
I ken douce reason bids me wheesht—
But, luve, the hert is cauld!
Yet throu the cauldrife dirl o skaith
That dings ma hert sae fell
There leams yir tyger glaummerie
I maun loo i the pit o hell.

(wersh - bitter, drumlie - roiled and muddy, bree - brew, skaith - wound,
ding - beat, gargoulls - goblins, gowl - howl, ahint - behind, stoundit -
stunned, douce - soft, cauldrife - freezing, dirl - pierce, dings - strikes,
glaummerie - glamor, maun - must, loo - love)

William Soutar

THE STAR

Whan my faither's faither was a bairn
Wi nocht but bairnly care
Yon haw-tree fleurin on the cairn
Had weather'd a hundred year.

And the hill was green abune its rock,
And the burn cam burblin doun,
Lang, lang, afore the hamely folk
Biggit our borough-toun.

And yon wee licht frae its lanely place
Glinted as cauld and clear
Whan nicht rov'd through this howe o' space
Afore a world was here.

BALLAD

O! shairly ye hae seen my love
Doun whaur the waters wind;
He walks like ane wha fears nae man
And yet his e'en are kind.

O! shairly ye hae seen my love
At the turnin' o' the tide;
For then he gethers in the nets
Doun by the waterside.

O! lassie I hae seen your love
At the turnin' o' the tide;
And he was wi' the fisher-folk
Doun by the waterside.

The fisher-folk were at their trade
No far from Walnut Grove;
They gether'd in their dreepin' nets
And found your ain true love.

THE GOWK

Half doun the hill where fa's the linn,
  Far frae the flaught of fowk,
I saw upon a lanely whin,
  A lanely singin' gowk!
    Cuckoo, cuckoo;
Behind my back
The howie hill stuid up and spak,
    Cuckoo, cuckoo.

There was nae soun', the loupin' linn
  Was frostit in its fa';
Nae bird was on the lanely whin
  Sae white with fleurs o' snaw,
    Cuckoo, cuckoo;
I stuid stane still
And gently spak the howie hill
    Cuckoo, cuckoo.

THE TRYST

O luely, luely, cam she in
And luely she lay doun:
I kent her be her caller lips
And her breists sae sma' and roun'.

A' thru the nicht we spak nae word
Nor sinder'd bane frae bane:
A' thru the nicht I heard her hert
Gang soundin' wi' my ain.

It was about the waukrife hour
When cocks begin to craw
That she smool'd saftly thru the mirk
Afore the day wud daw.

Sae luely, luely, cam she in
Saie luely was she gaen;
And wi' her a' my simmer days
Like they had never been.

WAIT FOR THE HOUR
(to a poet)

When day follows inarticulate day;
When the mind would speak
But the heart has nought to say—
Wait for the hour.
Wait for the hour
Nor fret against the sense
Which is more old, more wise than intelligence.
O thrust not forth your word
Like a driven bird
Which braves its fledgeling breast to the blasts of the air;
Which strains an awkward wing
To meet the spring
While yet the fields are broken and the boughs are bare.
Wait for the hour;
As, hoarded within the bud,
The leaves must wait if they would bear a flower:
As wait earth's waters till their strength can flood
Under the moon.
Wait for the hour:

It is not late nor soon,
But this your power—
To curb the fretful brain and trust the blood.

THE THOCHT

Young Janie was a strappin' lass
  Wha deid in jizzen-bed,
And monie a thocht her lover thocht
  Lang eftir she was dead;

But aye, wi' a' he brocht to mind
  O' misery and wrang,
There was a gledness gathered in
  Like the owercome o' a sang:

And, gin the deid are naethingness
  Or they be minded on,
As hinny to a hungry ghaist
  Maun be a thocht like yon.

(owercome - refrain; hinny - honey)

THE PERMANENCE OF THE YOUNG MEN

No man outlives the grief of war
Though he outlive its wreck:
Upon the memory a scar
Through all his years will ache.

Hope will revive when horrors cease;
And dreaming dread be stilled;

225

But there shall dwell within his peace
A sadness unannulled.

Upon his world shall hang a sign
Which summer cannot hide:
The permanence of the young men
Who are not by his side.

Bernard Spencer

AEGEAN ISLANDS 1940-41

Where white, stares, smokes or breaks,
Thread white, white of plaster and of foam,
Where sea like a wall falls;
Ribbed, lionish coast,
The stony islands which blow into my mind
More often than I imagine my grassy home;

To sun one's bones beside the
Explosive, crushed-blue, nostril-opening sea
(The weaving sea, splintered with sails and foam,
Familiar of famous and deserted harbours,
Of coins with dolphins on and fallen pillars.)

To know the gear and skill of sailing,
The drenching race for home and the sail-white houses,
Stories of Turks and smoky ikons,
Cry of the bagpipe, treading
Of the peasant dancers;

The dark bread
The island wine and the sweet dishes;
All these were elements in a happiness
More distant now than any date like '40,
A. D. or B. C., ever can express.

LETTERS

Letters, like blood along a weakening body
move fainter round our map. On dangerous wings,
on darkness-loving keels they go, so longed for;
but say no memorable things.

The "dear" and "darling" and the "yours for ever"
are relics of a style. But most appears
mere rambling notes; passion and tenderness
fall like a blot or a burst of tears.

Now public truths are scarcer currency,
what measure for the personal truth? how can
this ink and paper coursing continents
utter the clothed or the naked man?

A HAND

The human hand lying on my hand
(The wrist had a gilt bangle on)
Wore its print of personal lines
Took breath as lungs and leaves and
Tasted in the skin our sun.

The living palm and the near-to-bone:
Fine animal hairs where the light shone.

The handed mole to its earth, the stoat to the dark
And this flesh to its nature nervously planned;
To dig love's heart till everything is shown,
To hunt, to hold its mark
—This loved hand.

ILL

Expectant at the country gate the lantern. On the night
Its silks of light strained. Lighted upper window.
"Is it you who sent for me?" The two go in
To where the woman lies ill, upstairs, out of sight.

I hear sky softly smother to earth in rain,
As I sit by the controls and the car's burning dials.
And always the main-road traffic searching, searching the
    horizons.
Then those sounds knifed by the woman's Ah! of pain.

Who dreamed this; the dark folding murderer's hands round
    the lamps?
The rain blowing growth to rot? Lives passed beneath a
    ritual
That tears men's ghosts and bodies; the few healers
With their weak charms, moving here and there among the
    lamps?

Stephen Spender

A CHILDHOOD

I am glad I met you on the edge
Of your barbarous childhood

In what purity of pleasure
You danced alone like a peasant
For the stamping joy's own sake!

How, set in their sandy sockets,
Your clear, truthful, transparent eyes
Shone out of the black frozen landscape
Of those gray-clothed schoolboys!

How your shy hand offered
The total generosity
Of original unforewarned fearful trust,
In a world grown old in iron hatred!

I am glad to set down
The first and ultimate you,
Your inescapable soul. Although
It fade like a fading smile
Or light falling from faces
Which some grimmer preoccupation replaces.

This happens everywhere at every time:
Joy lacks the cause for joy,
Love the answering love,

And truth the objectless persistent loneliness,
As they grow older,
To become later what they were
In childhood earlier,—
In a world of cheating compromise.

Childhood, its own flower,
Flushes from the grasses with no reason
Except the sky of that season.
But the grown desires need objects
And taste of these corrupts the tongue
And the natural need is scattered
In satisfactions which satisfy
A debased need.

Yet all prayers are on the side of
Giving strength to naturalness,
So I pray for nothing new,
I pray only, after such knowledge,
That you may have the strength to be you.

And I shall remember
You who, being younger,
Will probably forget.

ON THE PILOTS WHO DESTROYED GERMANY IN THE SPRING OF 1945

I stood on a roof top and they wove their cage
Their murmuring throbbing cage, in the air of blue crystal.
I saw them gleam above the town like diamond bolts
Conjoining invisible struts of wire,

Carrying through the sky their geometric cage
Woven by senses delicate as a shoal of flashing fish.

They went. They left a silence in our streets below
Which boys gone to schoolroom leave in their playground.
A silence of asphalt, of privet hedge, of staring wall.
In the glass emptied sky their diamonds had scratched
Long curving finest whitest lines.
These the day soon melted into satin ribbons
Falling over heaven's terraces near the golden sun.

Oh that April morning they carried my will
Exalted expanding singing in their aeriel cage.
They carried my will. They dropped it on a German town.
My will expanded and tall buildings fell down.

Then, when the ribbons faded and the sky forgot,
And April was concerned with building nests and being hot
I began to remember the lost names and faces.

Now I tie the ribbons torn down from those terraces
Around the most hidden image in my lines,
And my life, which never paid the price of their wounds,
Turns thoughts over and over like a propellor
Assumes their guilt, honours, repents, prays for them.

THE LABOURER IN THE VINEYARD

Here are the ragged towers of vines
Stepped down the slope in terraces.

Through torn spaces between spearing leaves
The lake glows with waters combed sideways,

And climbing up to reach the vine-spire vanes
The mountain crests beyond the far shore
Paint their sky of glass with rocks and snow.

Lake below, mountains above, between
Turrets of leaves, grape-triangles, the labourer stands.

His tanned trousers form a pedestal,
Coarse tree-trunk rising from the earth with bark
Peeled away at the navel to show
Shining torso of sun-burnished god
Breast of lyre, mouth coining song.

My ghostly, passing-by thoughts gather
Around his hilly shoulders, like those clouds
Around those mountain peaks their transient scrolls.

He is the classic writing all this day,
Through his mere physical being focussing
All into nakedness. His hand
With outspread fingers is a star whose rays
Concentrate timeless inspiration
Onto the god descended in a vineyard
With hand unclenched against the lake's taut sail
Flesh filled with statue, as the grape with wine.

ON THE THIRD DAY

On the first summer day I lay in the valley.
Above rocks the sky sealed my eyes with a leaf
The grass licked my skin. The flowers bound my nostrils
With scented cotton threads. The soil invited
My hands and feet to grow down and have roots.

232

Bees and grass-hoppers drummed over
Crepitations of thirst rising from dry stones,
And the ants rearranged my ceaseless thoughts
Into different patterns for ever the same.
Then the blue wind fell out of the air
And the sun hammered down till I became of wood
Glistening brown beginning to warp.

On the second summer day I climbed through the forest's
Huge tent pegged to the mountain-side by roots.
My direction was cancelled by that great sum of trees.
Here darkness lay under the leaves in a war
Against light, which occasionally penetrated
Splintering spears through several interstices
And dropping white clanging shields on the soil.
Silence was stitched through with thinnest pine needles
And bird songs were stifled behind a hot hedge.
My feet became as heavy as logs.
I drank up all the air of the forest.
My mind changed to amber transfixed with dead flies.

On the third summer day I sprang from the forest
Into the wonder of a white snow-tide.
Alone with the sun's wild whispering wheel,
Grinding seeds of secret light on frozen fields,
Every burden fell from me, the forest from my back,
The valley dwindled to bewildering visions
Seen through torn shreds of the sailing clouds.
Above the snowfield one rock against the sky
Shaped out of pure silence a naked tune
Like a violin when the tune forsakes the instrument
And the pure sound flies through the ears' gate
And a whole sky floods the pool of one mind.

233

O NIGHT O TREMBLING NIGHT

O night O trembling night O night of sighs
O night when my body was a rod O night
When my mouth was a vague animal cry
Pasturing on her flesh O night
When the close darkness was a nest
Made of her hair and filled with my eyes

(O stars impenetrable above
The fragile tent poled with our thighs
Among the petals falling fields of time
O night revolving all our dark away)

O day O gradual day O sheeted light
Covering her body as with dews
Until I brushed her sealing sleep away
To read once more in the uncurtained day
Her naked love, my great good news.

Derek Stanford

THE TOMB OF HONEY SNAPS ITS MARBLE CHAINS

"*J'écris seulement pour vous exalter.*" — Guillaume Apollinaire

    Year after year before my life began
I lived with lug-worms in a sunken marsh.
Feet of the town stamped over me by day:
clocks of the town above me chimed at night.

    Fossil among the gutters of the world,
I grew like cactus in a pavement's crack;

234

cigarette-ash and excrement my food,
urine of dogs and rain moistened my mouth.

My head was bent,
my lips were glued to earth;
boots strode upon the gang-plank of my neck;
beetles filed through the postern of my teeth
and scurried down the lift-shaft of my throat.

Darkness, the taste of sourness, choking dust,
the insane speech of dynasties of mice;
Time in his own asylum faintly raving,
contriving wreaths of slime-dank silver daisies,
kissing his luminous finger-tips to Death.

The arrogance of haughty high-heeled shoes,
the chain-gang trudge of a multitude of slaves
forged an iron echo in my shackled skull.
The moon's infected spittle lay in my hair.

How can I write of the buried will's revolt,
that vast protracted midnight of rebellion
when the heart cracks like the sepulchre of a god,
and Time and Fate—earth's hypocritical mourners—
freeze into standing shadows,
and resurrection
grapples and shatters its pre-determined shell?

So I was born in an avalanche of carnage,
torn from the jailor-image of my heart,
severed in pain from the double of all my durance:
reeking with crimsoned sweat I stood complete.

235

How can I speak of the trumpets and the garlands,
giant hands that tended me sheathed in gloves of flowers;
choirs, beyond stars, proclaiming through the ether
"Only the Free shall discover the Morning River;
only the Free who are pure shall uncover My Face,"

I drank the Milky Way's sweet foaming cordial
fresh from the spouting nipples of the sky.
Now I walk upright, crowned with the bee's gold halo;
sure-footed as a panther, shod with fern.

For those who slake their thirst at the constellations,
who wear their love like a sprig of mistle-toe,
the Spring shall be a never-failing garden,
and bread shall be "a star upon the tongue."

CAROL FOR HIS DARLING ON CHRISTMAS DAY

Tonight the Christmas landscape of the skull
throngs brightly with white images of angels
like parallel ropes of pearl, poised above spires,
surmounting towers, ascending and descending.

Streets, squares, and gardens of the tired heart's town
receive snow-wise the promise of this song,
shuttling its theme like a glinting row of beads
between the icy earth and the granite sky.

Christ, sing the voices like uplifted candles,
is born anew in memory's dim manger,
warmed by the friendly incense of the oxen;
miraculous and immaculate as snow.

The unrejoicing heart has resurrection;
joy burns in the air like an incandescent star.
But this is a story for our private theatre:
outside, the night is dank and uninspired.

Down by the shore the wave repeats its secret
of banal worth to the uninterested sand,
and here the senile ash in the funeral fire
utters its grey disintegrating sigh.

Darling, accept these symbols of thanksgiving,
these blanched and shining signs of blessedness,
these jubilations of the lonely night-time,
these holly rites of a happy imagination.

It was your love designed this festival:
your love I feel as an ether-weighted flake,
as the shy white Christmas snow that falls in mye heart,
stroking its dales with a tingling finger of peace.

Julian Symons

SPRING POEM

The muscles flex, contract,
Over the sprouting garden,
The blood moves to shade from
Faces this burning sun,
Running and roaring spring
Permits me to say thanks
Now the bent arm includes
You with the cooing pigeons.

237

The arm takes in its sweep
The strengthening light the flowers
And the hard touch of love,
Not asking what is ready
Or wishing what is good
Is aware only of slow
Movement of the body
We shall possess, not keep.

We know little of good
And that little goes away,
But the sad human heart
Must always wish for joy,
For the face like alabaster
Which is breathing and warm
And the arm falling like velvet
On the opposing arm.

Minutes will move and brush
This season from the hand,
The year moves on to worse
Than we have ever known,
But uncritical this moment
I give thanks for the drug
That turns two into one,
Making casual the eye,
Stopping the mind's deceit,
Letting the arm select
You with the flowers and pigeons.

FOR MY WIFE

Sitting at evening in the warm grass
I look at the barracks cradled between hills.
Purring along the sky the fighters pass.
A daze of heat fills
Up my mind against the usual fears.
I think of these last two years

Stamped permanently upon our wavering lives.
I think of you. The very face of love
Speaks, and tells me what love gives:
This power to see and move
Outside ourselves, these trees and this green view:
As I, alone and idle here, see you,

So easily laughing and so quickly happy
Or quickly sad, for whom the natural
Events of life are tidal like the sea:
For whom the world is all
Simple, made up exclusively of people:
Now, although each church steeple

Reveals the power of idols, every action
Involves its opposite and must disclose
A painful birth of bureaucratic faction,
Today when every rose
Shows up its worm, I more than ever preserve
This radical and single love we serve.

And I present this love now as a symbol
Of our best hopes, and weigh this good we've known
Against the times when we betray and dissemble;

Now in this place alone
I offer unaffected thanks that we,
In spite of our time, being together are happy.

And in the future that we move towards, I trust
That whatever fails at least this may survive
As compensation for our end of dust,
This love, that is alive
And vivid in a world of falsehood,
That, where so much is doubtful, certainly is good.

HOMAGE TO OUR LEADERS

These larger-than-life comic characters,
Churchill the moonface moocow chewing
A permanent cigar, Roosevelt the gigantic
False Liberal mask with syrup smile,
Medicine-man Stalin like Aunt Sally at a fair,
All snapping like canvas in the wind...

Our world, our time, our murder
Evolved these monsters: who like the allosaurus
Should be remembered as a stupidity
We have outgrown. Now they sprawl across
Hoardings, papers, radios, these simple shapeless demons.
Friend, lock your door at night: watch neighbour and wife,
See that your eyes are hidden behind dark glasses,
Remember that you live by permission of the police.

Dylan Thomas

POEM

Especially when the October wind
With frosty fingers punishes my hair,
Caught by the crabbing sun I walk on fire
And cast a shadow crab upon the land,
By the sea's side, hearing the noise of birds,
Hearing the raven cough in winter sticks,
My busy heart who shudders as she talks
Sheds the syllabic blood and drains her words.

Shut, too, in a tower of words, I mark
On the horizon walking like the trees
The wordy shapes of women, and the rows
Of the star-gestured children in the park.
Some let me make you of the vowelled beeches,
Some of the oaken voices, from the roots
Of many a thorny shire tell you notes,
Some let me make you of the water's speeches.

Behind a pot of ferns the wagging clock
Tells me the hour's word, the neural meaning
Flies on the shafted disc, declaims the morning
And tells the windy weather in the cock.
Some let me make you of the meadow's signs;
The signal grass that tells me all I know
Breaks with the wormy winter through the eye.
Some let me tell you of the raven's sins.

Especially when the October wind
(Some let me make you of autumnal spells,
The spider-tongued, and the loud hill of Wales)
With fist of turnips punishes the land,
Some let me make you of the heartless words.
The heart is drained that, spelling in the scurry
Of chemic blood, warned of the coming fury.
By the sea's side hear the dark-vowelled birds.

POEM

A process in the weather of the heart
Turns damp to dry; the golden shot
Storms in the freezing tomb.
A weather in the quarter of the veins
Turns night to day; blood in their suns
Lights up the living worm.

A process in the eye forewarns
The bones of blindness; and the womb
Drives in a death as life leaks out.

A darkness in the weather of the eye
Is half its light; the fathomed sea
Breaks on unangled land.
The seed that makes a forest of the loin
Forks half its fruit; and half drops down,
Slow in a sleeping wind.

A weather in the flesh and bone
Is damp and dry; the quick and dead
Move like two ghosts before the eye.

A process in the weather of the world
Turns ghost to ghost; each mothered child
Sits in their double shade.
A process blows the moon into the sun,
Pulls down the shabby curtains of the skin;
And the heart gives up its dead.

IN MEMORY OF ANN JONES

After the funeral, mule praises, brays,
Windshake of sailshaped ears, muffle-toed tap
Tap happily of one peg in the thick
Grave's foot, blinds down the lids, the teeth in black,
The spittled eyes, the salt ponds in the sleeves,
Morning smack of the spade that wakes up sleep,
Shakes a desolate boy who slits his throat
In the dark of the coffin and sheds dry leaves,
That breaks one bone to light with a judgment clout,
After the feast of tear-stuffed time and thistles
In a room with a stuffed fox and a stale fern,
I stand, for this memorial's sake, alone
In the snivelling hours with dead, humped Ann
Whose hooded, fountain heart once fell in puddles
Round the parched worlds of Wales and drowned each sun
(Though this for her is a monstrous image blindly
Magnified out of praise; her death was a still drop;
She would not have me sinking in the holy
Flood of her heart's fame; she would lie dumb and deep
And need no druid of her broken body).
But I, Ann's bard on a raised hearth, call all
The seas to service that her wood-tongued virtue
Babble like a bellbuoy over the hymning heads,

Bow down the walls of the ferned and foxy woods
That her love sing and swing through a brown chapel,
Bless her bent spirit with four, crossing birds.
Her flesh was meek as milk, but this skyward statue
With the wild breast and blessed and giant skull
Is carved from her in a room with a wet window
In a fiercely mourning house in a crooked year.
I know her scrubbed and sour humble hands
Lie with religion in their cramp, her threadbare
Whisper in a damp word, her wits drilled hollow,
Her fist of a face died clenched on a round pain;
And sculptured Ann is seventy years of stone.
These cloud-sopped, marble hands, this monumental
Argument of the hewn voice, gesture and psalm
Storm me forever over her grave until
The stuffed lung of the fox twitch and cry Love
And the strutting fern lay seeds on the black sill.

AND DEATH SHALL HAVE NO DOMINION

And death shall have no dominion.
Dead men naked they shall be one
With the man in the wind and the west moon;
When their bones are picked clean and the clean bones gone,
They shall have stars at elbow and foot;
Though they go mad they shall be sane,
Though they sink through the sea they shall rise again;
Though lovers be lost love shall not;
And death shall have no dominion.

And death shall have no dominion.
Under the windings of the sea

They lying long shall not die windily;
Twisting on racks when sinews give way,
Strapped to a wheel, yet they shall not break;
Faith in their hands shall snap in two,
And the unicorn evils run them through;
Split all ends up they shan't crack;
And death shall have no dominion.

And death shall have no dominion.
No more may gulls cry at their ears
Or waves break loud on the seashores;
Where blew a flower may a flower no more
Lift its head to the blows of the rain;
Though they be made and dead as nails,
Heads of the characters hammer through daisies;
Break in the sun till the sun breaks down,
And death shall have no dominion.

IN MY CRAFT OR SULLEN ART

In my craft or sullen art
Exercised in the still night
When only the moon rages
And the lovers lie abed
With all their griefs in their arms,
I labour by singing light
Not for ambition or bread
Or the strut and trade of charms
On the ivory stages
But for the common wages
Of their most secret heart.

Not for the proud man apart
From the raging moon I write
On these spindrift pages
Not for the towering dead
With their nightingales and psalms
But for the lovers, their arms
Round the griefs of the ages,
Who pay no praise or wages
Nor heed my craft or art.

POEM IN OCTOBER

It was my thirtieth year to heaven
Woke to my hearing from harbour and neighbour wood
And the mussel pooled and the heron
Priested shore
The morning beckon
With water praying and call of seagull and rook
And the knock of sailing boats on the net webbed wall
Myself to set foot
That second
In the still sleeping town and set forth.

My birthday began with the water—
Birds and the birds of the winged trees flying my name
Above the farms and the white horses
And I rose
In rainy autumn
And walked abroad in a shower of all my days.
High tide and the heron dived when I took the road
Over the border
And the gates
Of the town closed as the town awoke.

A springful of larks in a rolling
Cloud and the roadside bushes brimming with whistling
Blackbirds and the sun of October
Summery
On the hill's shoulder,
Here were fond climates and sweet singers suddenly
Come in the morning where I wandered and listened
To the rain wringing
Wind blow cold
In the wood faraway under me.

Pale rain over the dwindling harbour
And over the sea wet church the size of a snail
With its horns through mist and the castle
Brown as owls,
But all the gardens
Of spring and summer were blooming in the tall tales
Beyond the border and under the lark full cloud.
There could I marvel
My birthday
Away but the weather turned around.

It turned away from the blithe country
And down the other air and the blue altered sky
Streamed again a wonder of summer
With apples
Pears and red currants
And I saw in the turning so clearly a child's
Forgotten mornings when he walked with his mother
Through the parables
Of sun light
And the legends of the green chapels.

247

And the twice told fields of infancy
That his tears burned my cheeks and his heart moved in mine.
These were the woods the river and sea
Where a boy
In the listening
Summertime of the dead whispered the truth of his joy
To the trees and the stones and the fish in the tide.
And the mystery
Sang alive
Still in the water and singing birds.

And there could I marvel my birthday
Away but the weather turned around. And the true
Joy of the long dead child sang burning
In the sun.
It was my thirtieth
Year to heaven stood there then in the summer noon
Though the town below lay leaved with October blood.
O may my heart's truth
Still be sung
On this high hill in a year's turning.

POEM

The force that through the green fuse drives the flower
Drives my green age; that blasts the roots of trees
Is my destroyer.
And I am dumb to tell the crooked rose
My youth is bent by the same wintry fever.

The force that drives the water through the rocks
Drives my red blood; that dries the mouthing streams

Turns mine to wax.
And I am dumb to mouth unto my veins
How at the mountain spring the same mouth sucks.

The hand that whirls the water in the pool
Stirs the quicksand; that ropes the blowing wind
Hauls my shroud sail.
And I am dumb to tell the hanging man
How of my clay is made the hangman's lime.

The lips of time leech to the fountain head;
Love drips and gathers, but the fallen blood
Shall calm her sores.
And I am dumb to tell a weather's wind
How time has ticked a heaven round the stars.

And I am dumb to tell the lover's tomb   .
How at my sheet hoes the same crooked worm.

A REFUSAL TO MOURN THE DEATH, BY FIRE, OF
  A CHILD IN LONDON

Never until the mankind making
Bird beast and flower
Fathering and all humbling darkness
Tells with silence the last light breaking
And the still hour
Is come of the sea tumbling in harness

And I must enter again the round
Zion of the water bead
And the synagogue of the ear of corn

249

Shall I let pray the shadow of a sound
Or sow my salt seed
In the least valley of sackcloth to mourn

The majesty and burning of the child's death.
I shall not murder
The mankind of her going with a grave truth
Nor blaspheme down the stations of the breath
With any further
Elegy of innocence and youth.

Deep with the first dead lies London's daughter,
Robed in the long friends,
The grains beyond age, the dark veins of her mother
Secret by the unmourning water
Of the riding Thames.
After the first death, there is no other.

Terence Tiller

NO TIME

You will not see the sorrow of no time.
There will be birds bearing rings, ravens; hands
with an empty hourglass and a sword.
Things half-seen in a familiar room
will rise against you. These will be dangerous friends.
You will not see the sorrow of no time
Or singing burst your melancholy cord.

In days of nightingales, and when our streets
are all nostalgic turnings, and the west

a broken harbour, there will be terror walking.
You will not know the crossing of our hearts,
the final stake that burrows through the breast.
The cruel delicious voices of the birds
will be silent for you. For you unwaking.

Then all my journeys will be bellman-like,
a wanderer in your city crying hours.
Call me the raven friend: that cry will come.
There will be nothing in the opened book
but evil spoken. These are the hollowed years.
Death in the longing way begins to walk.

You will not see the sorrow of no time.

PROTHALAMION

The instant splendour, the swung bells that speak
once to the unprepared glory of youth;
     then the bewildering care:
and nothing more but the stag's backward look,
and the approach of all we were.

And this is the key of the kingdom. Oh my love,
there was a time when the blue-feathered sky,
     the gilded haughty trees,
clad the sardonic rook in the voice of the dove;
when homeward streets were palaces,

and earth was the delight held in a child's hand.
We shook the door, stretched our hands out to the key;
     years closed behind. And yet

we shall not lose that age; it is the hound;
we turn and hear his steady feet.

Over our human purpose winds go
round the unpeopled spaces of the night;
    this night, when we shall join
under their swaying canopy, we know
our heart shall be a child's again.

For they have blown, and the blind stag has fled,
through our perfecting years. The kingdom comes
    though by a narrow gate.
To snare his antlers in his native wood,
the stag runs gladly, soon or late.

This love shall fill the sky again with wings,
and the trees' proud enamel of sunlight be
    as when our eyes were gods'.
Here is the ghostly glory, and the bell swings
here, in the mingling of our bloods.

THE END OF THE STORY

Put out the candle, close the biting rose,
for cock and cony are asleep; the sheep
in her secretive hills, with fleece at peace,
now lies enfolded.

The hungry sceptre-kissing mouth, the moth
behind the fingers, no more eat the night;
the rooting worm has crawled away from play
in his wet burrows.

Now the extremest joys are dreams and toys;
it's darkness in a vast full-tide abed;
over abandoned bodies time shall climb
like the black spider.

Give memory all amazing hours, all showers
or sharply pouring seas between the knees;
slack as a rope, the flesh is dull, and full
of its perfection.

And all that lately flashed and leapt is gripped
into a knot of symbols; all's grown small,
quiet as curtains: brave be this your grave,
and fresh your garlands.

BATHERS

They flutter out of white, and run
through the electric wind to bathe,
giggling like rivers for the fun
of smacking mud in the toes, of lithe
and sliding bodies like their own
—sharp rushes, good to battle with.

The child knows all delight to be
naked and queer as his own name,
foreign as being loved; but he
feels as a kind of coming home
the flags that slap his plunging knee,
and the cold stocking of the stream.

Coiling in wombs of water, bent
backwards upon the sheets of air,
his wand of sexless body lent
to all that was or casts before,
he strips to either element
a foetus or a ravisher.

So gladly virgin rivers rush
down to their amniotic seas,
children of cold and glittering flesh
that promise harvest as they pass
panics of tiny fertile fish
in the fast pale of boisterous thighs.

KILLED IN ACTION

They know the lion's power,
being now indifferent,
whose eager limbs have learnt
to suffer without fear
or consoling love
the bridal and the bed
of the unearthly dead.

They lie in beds of love
with worn and vivid face,
where fall in one embrace
the dead by the alive
the carnal by the just,
being now indifferent
to lust or monument.

They have all grown just,
as mindless change or growth
—animal life and death,
blind blood of trees, thrust
of the innocent spray
and the pitiless flower:
they know the lion's power.

IMAGE IN A LILAC TREE

Tireless budding and flowering of women
to a child and a child; the closed evening-care
of motherhood: from what slim boughs the lilac
swells into lavender torches, the flesh
blooms through its leaves!

Or now the heart is heavy and sweet with words,
and a great wind sways the tongue: oh eloquence
of gardens bursting through the narrow pen
into five senses, that clutch beauty as
a child the breast!

The lilac's evening-coloured breasts of smoke,
bare like a Cretan lady's to the firm
poetic moonlight: love, conception, birth,
where the five tongues of living drink, and are
poem and image.

Ruthven Todd

WATCHING YOU WALK

(For N)

Watching you walk slowly across a stage,
Suddenly I am become aware of all the past;
Of all the tragic queens and maids of every age,
Of Joan, whose love the flames could not arrest;

Of those to whom always love was the first duty,
Who saw behind the crooked world the ugly and weak,
Whose kindliness was no gesture; no condescending pity
Could rule their actions; those whom Time broke,

But whom he could not totally destroy.
Hearing the truth you give to these dead words,
Whose writer feared the life they might enjoy,
I can recall the mating orchestra of birds

Behind your voice, as lying by the lake,
You read me poems, and I, too deeply moved,
Watched the swans for a moment, before I spoke
The trivialities, unable to tell you how I loved.

Watching your fingers curl about a painted death,
I am suddenly glad that it is April, that you are queen
Of all the sordid marches of my bruised heart,
That, loving you, the poplars never seemed so green;

Glad of my lonely walk beside the shrunken river,
Thinking of you while seeing the tufts of ash,

The chestnut candles and unreal magnolia's wax flower;
Glad that, in loving you, the whole world lives afresh.

SIX WINTERS

Six winters since, I dandled on my knee
The neat-tholed toy that was my son,
That yet was more than toy and more to me
Than all the herodian innocents rolled in one,
Or that child whose mother fled by the Egyptian sea.

Now I am gallows where no mandrake grows,
No bryony twines up my splintering grey shaft;
Though hanging history creaks as the gale blows,
My sole possessions are the leaves that drift
This sodden autumn, waiting cementing snows:

Or else my fancy says I am explorer still,
Haunting the fringes of a never travelled land,
The hypochondriac dreamer, torn by an untrue ill,
Who dare not drop the guide-book from his hand,
Nor venture more than eye's length from the closest hill.

For these six winters of a war which stole
This that I loved so much, have also taken
Much that my time thought good, thought real,
Been X-ray shewing the diagnostic much mistaken,
Disclosed the gentle hand grown horned and cruel.

257

TO A VERY BEAUTIFUL LADY

(For U)

And when you walk the world lifts up its head,
Planets are haloed by the unembarassed stars,
The town lies fallow at your feet, the ancient dead
Recall their loves, their queens and emperors,
Their shepherds and the quiet pastoral scene.
For less than you Troy burned and Egypt fell,
The corn was blasted while it still stood green
And Faustus went protesting into hell.

Be careful, sweet, adored by half your world,
Time to its darlings is not always kind—
There lie the lovelies whom the years have scored
Deeper than all the hearts which once repined.
The knife you hold could cut an empire low,
Or in your own breast place the suicidal blow.

PERSONAL HISTORY: FOR MY SON

O my heart is the unlucky heir of the ages
And my body is unwillingly the secret agent
Of my ancestors; those content with their wages
From history: the Cumberland Quaker whose gentle
Face was framed with lank hair to hide the ears
Cropped as a punishment for his steadfast faith,
The Spanish lady who had seen the pitch lake's broth
In the West Indian island and the Fife farmers
To whom the felted barley meant a winter's want.

258

My face presents my history, and its sallow skin
Is parchment for the Edinburgh lawyer's deed:
To have and hold in trust, as feeofee therein
Until such date as the owner shall have need
Thereof. My brown eyes are jewels I cannot pawn,
And my long lip once curled beside an Irish bog,
My son's whorled ear was once my father's, then mine;
I am the map of a campaign, each ancestor has his flag
Marking an advance or a retreat. I am their seed.

As I write I look at the five fingers of my hand,
Each with its core of nacre bone, and rippled nails;
Turn to the palm and the traced unequal lines that end
In death—only at the tips my ancestry fails—
The dotted swirls are original, and are my own:
Look at the fringed polyp which I daily use
And ask its history, ask to what grave abuse
It has been put: perhaps it curled about the stone
Of Cain. At least it has known much of evil.

And perhaps as much of good, been tender
When tenderness was needed, and been firm
On occasion, and in its past been free of gender,
Been the hand of a mother holding the warm
Impress of the child against her throbbing breast,
Been cool to the head inflamed in fever,
Sweet and direct in contact with a lover.
O in its cupped and fluted shell lies all the past,
My fingers close about the crash of history's storm.

In the tent of night I hear the voice of Calvin
Expending his hatred of the world in icy words;

259

Man less than a red ant beneath the towering mountain,
And God a troll more fearful than the feudal lords:
The Huguenots in me, flying Saint Bartholomew's Day,
Are in agreement with all this, and their resentful hate
Flames brighter than the candles on an altar, the grey
Afternoon is lit by Catherine wheels of terror, the street
Drinks blood and pity is death before their swords.

The cantilever of my bones acknowledges the architect,
My father, to whom always the world was a mystery
Concealed in the humped base of a bottle, one solid fact
To set against the curled pages and the tears of history.
I am a Border keep, a croft and a solicitor's office,
A country rectory, a farm and a drawing board:
In me, as in so many, the past has stowed its miser's hoard,
Won who knows where nor with what loaded dice.
When my blood pulses it is their blood I feel hurry.

These forged me, the latest link in a fertile chain,
With ends that run so far that my short sight
Cannot follow them, nor can my weak memory claim
Acquaintance with the earliest shackle. In my height
And breadth I hold history, and then my son
Holds my history in his small body and the history of another,
Who for me has no contact but that of flesh, his mother.
What I make now I make, indeed, from the unknown,
A blind man spinning furiously in the web of night.

VARIOUS ENDS

Sidney, according to report, was kindly hearted
When stretched upon the field of death;

And in his gentleness, ignored the blood that spurted,
Expending the last gutter of his flickering breath.

Marlowe, whose raw temper used to rise
Like boiling milk, went on the booze;
A quick word and his half-startled eyes
Mirrored his guts flapping on his buckled shoes.

Swift went crazy in his lonely tower,
Where blasphemous obscenity paid the warders,
Who brought a string of visitors every hour
To see the wild beast, the Dean in holy orders.

And there were those who coughed out their sweet soft lungs
Upon the mountains, or the clear green sea.
Owen found half-an-ounce of lead with wings;
And Tennyson died quietly, after tea.

Sam Johnson scissored at the surgeon's stitches
To drain more poison from his bloated body.
And Bryon may have recalled the pretty bitches,
Nursing his fevered head in hands unsteady.

De Nerval finished swinging from a grid
And round his neck the Queen of Sheba's garter.
Swinburne died of boredom, doing as he was bid,
And Shelley bobbed lightly on the Mediterranean water.

Rimbaud, his leg grown blue and gross and round,
Lay sweating for those last weeks on his truckle-bed;
He could not die—the future was unbroken ground—
Only Paris, Verlaine and poetry were dead.

261

Blake had no doubts, his old fingers curled
Around dear Kate's frail and transparent hand;
Death merely meant a changing of his world,
A widening of experience, for him it marked no end.

THE LONELY MONTH

(For J)

This long and lonely month
With memory nagging like a broken gramophone,
Evenings devoted to darts and too much beer,
The early morning rising,
The battering awkwardly upon the typewriter
And the planting of strange seeds.
This long and lonely month.

This long and lonely month
With the emptiness full of fluff and feathers,
The silent house driving me out to walk
Alone along these Essex lanes,
Or to hoe the persistent weeds,
The nettles and the thistles that push up
Inevitably through the month.

O yes, the yellow rock-rose
Shews its wafer petals, and the scabious
Buttons the roadsides, and the strawberry
Ripens, and young apples fall.
Yes, the sad prisoners thin the beet
And the cuckoo presses on the ear,
This long and lonely month...

This long and lonely month
Cannot efface my visual memories,
My last glance back before that corner
Cut like a razor blade.
Nor can I forget the small shadow
Sliding away along the western sky,
This long and lonely month.

This long and lonely month,
My love, had altered nothing in my heart;
In a far country, you, too, are lonely,
And these lines I write you now
Send you my love and tell you that I myself
Have been lonely as a leper,
This long and lonely month.

Henry Treece

POEM

In the dark caverns of the night,
Loveless and alone,
Friendless as wind that wails across the plains,
I sit, the last man left on earth,
Putting my fear on paper,
Praying that love will flow from my dry pen
And watching the tears make havoc on my page.

And I remember then,
Under the night's still mask,
The gallant geese
Making their way through storms,

263

The fieldmouse scuttering to my door
Away from the black cloud,
And the gay snail
Garnishing the twig before leaves came.

The old ones told me,
"When you grow grey you think on little things;"
Now these dreams kiss the bruises from my mind
Under the night's still mask,
As loveless and alone
I sit, till dawn the last man left
Who knows the sound of rain on summer leaves,
The graceful swan breasting the blood-red stream,
And heart's incompetence.

POEM

Death walks through the mind's dark woods,
Beautiful as aconite,
A lily-flower in his pale hand
And eyes like moonstones burning bright.

Love walks down heart's corridors
Singing for a crust of bread
All the tales of laughing youth
Who tomorrow will lie dead.

Here two summer metaphors;
For even on a sun-mad day
Laughter breaks into salt tears,
And grave is never far away.

POEM

Through the dark aisles of the wood
Where the pine-needles deaden all sound
And the dove flutters in the black boughs

Through twilit vaults of the forest
Where fungus stifles the roots
And the squirrel escapes with a cone

Through the dim alleys of pine
Where the bent stick moves like a snake
And the badger sniffs at the moon

Through the green graveyard of leaves
Where the stoat rehearses his kill
And the white skull grins in the fern.

THE WAITING WATCHERS

They shall come in the black weathers
From the heart of the dead embers,
Walking one and two over the hill.
And they shall be with you, never farther
Than your bedside.
                    At their will
The smell of putrefaction lingers
And floor is carpetted with rotting hair;
Or sheets are torn to shreds
                    By the beaks of dead dry birds
And the red blood clots in your cup.
                    Put up your swords!

265

What steel can cut the throat of next year's dream,
What tongue is tunes to speak last night's quick scream?
Go alone by darkness;
                    Burn the clippings of your nail;
Donate a thousand candles.
                    But do as you will,
When sun is blind and lamps are lit once more,
Two and one, they shall be standing
                    At your door.

THE HAUNTED GARDEN

In this sad place
Memory hangs on the air
Fragile as Spring snail's tiny shell,
Coming to the sympathetic ear
Gentle as bud's green pulsing in the sun,
Suave as sin in a black velvet glove;

The old faces gaze
Wistfully as birds, among the nodding leaves,
They watch the pleasures they may never share;
And through the twilight hours
Old voices call along the river banks,
And out of the high-walled garden.

Why do they sigh,
The gentle ones in the flowering musk;
And what are the words of the song
The pale stranger sings as he walks
The garden's still, deserted paths,
Like a boy searching for his dog?

John Waller

THE ENEMY

One night I held all Europe in my arms
And all the East, Asia and Africa.
Limbs were their armies, those easy lips
Their long grey fleets breathing of threat
And doom, even each whisper seemed
An airman gliding on his swallow path.

That was a conflict and a peace in one;
Holding each other fast, gay enemies
Then mad with love. The joyful passionate evening
Was declaration of war or armistice, just how
You choose to think. In the still night
The hotel room cradled us into sleep.

Now in the empty days I feel the loss
Of this illusion. Dull faces swarm
Over the seven seas and old men
Nod at the moon—emptiness is like that—
While somewhere preparing another war
You charm and entangle, merrily captivate.

WHEN SADNESS FILLS A JOURNEY

When sadness fills a journey
There is no last remorse
Between accepted ending
And the final turn we pass
To other sights or heroes

Or hunger in the cold
Fine air of morning sadness
Where all limbs must grow old.

So now I wear your picture
Against my heart for love
And know that you will wander
Across no lonely path,
But as a brighter darling,
A warm guest for the night,
Cry still: "My dearest favour
Is not so easily caught."

You, as the hour's enchanter,
Made circles as you would,
Posing a tricky charmer
Uncharmed but not withstood,
So wear this song for parting,
A gay song for the day
When limbs and charm and favour
Are warm but worn away.

LEGEND

Yesterday it seems you were acting on a stage
Yet so many years ago, so many years
I have heard the hooves of the horses racing
Through early mornings and thought of Antony
When his god left him at Alexandria sleeping

So, like Cavafy, dreamt of evenings and lights,
Laughter amid perils, the young not to return

From the ominous sands, a thought stained with laughter
Or lights, lights, the king cried, lights to forget
The dark, only your mood was softer

Was soft as the quicksilver running along limbs
That must always express, crying out from the sea
So certain never to be lost, a permanent pose
But soft as a kitten's, graceful as a gazelle's
Impatience for swiftness, light on the toes

And so waking again on an early morning
While the air from the window is cool, so cool
The years have passed I have thought to save
From that time your picture, for you were the first of
All my legendary people, first of the brave.

Cairo, June, 1945.

LIMB AND MIND

The disingenuous
Charm of living
Has its advantages
Properly using
Lips for smiling,
Grace for posture,
Limbs for loving,
Inimitable gesture.

The thinker enjoys
A lonelier quality,
Learning's shyness
With philosophy's pity,
The buried city

Of Troy or Babylon
Lost in antiquity,
Though breathing on.

Heart will answer
For limb's liveliness,
Brain will wonder
In mind's timelessness.
O frozen dress
Or whirlwind hero,
All gentleness,
All lust like Nero?

The ponderous question
Cleaves the lives
Of the moral rebel
And the constant loves.
So the limb strives
To the mind's derision
And the mind drives
To the lovers' schism.

Vernon Watkins

THE MUMMY

His eyes are closed. They are closed. His eyes are closed.
His hands are clenched. They are clenched. His hands are
clenched.
The messenger comes. The letters are disciplined; they are
disposed.
The black light quivers. Earth on Earth is avenged.

What has left music fast in the sockets of bone?
Had all been pattern, images sight had seen,
Blood would lie quiet, but something strokes the light, and
  a groan
Of great-rooted calm repels those images: nothing they mean.

Nothing here lives but the music in the eyes.
Hunting-scene, warriors, chariot, palm and wing
Bid the blood rest, thought perch where the time-bird sings
  or flies,
Year chasing year, following and following.

But tears wash these bones where parchments whisper to sand.
Here a laid vase offers the flying stream.
Sand darkening wakes a harp-string hidden, plucked by a blind
  hand,
Crying this theme to the world, this world-surrounding theme:

Valiant, alive, his voice pursued the lands,
Ruled the white sea, held mountains in his keep.
Leave him with delicate instruments formed for delicate hands;
In this locked room of treasures let him who chose them sleep.

I lean down, crying: "Touch me, lay hold on my Spring,
Reach up, for I have loosened, tearing your skies,
Fountains of light, ages of listening!"
But the bound hands are folded, the fold its word denies.

What shudder of music unfulfilled vibrates?
What draws to a dust-grain's fall most distant stars?
In the last taper's light what shadow meditates?
What single, athletic shape never cast on wall or vase?

271

What shudder of birth and death? What shakes me most?
Job his Maker answering, the Stricken exclaiming "Rejoice!"
Gripping late in the shifting moment giant Earth, making
  Earth a ghost,
Who heard a great friend's death without a change of voice.

YEATS' TOWER

Surely the finger of God that governs the stars
And feels the flashed mystery of the moving world
Stirring the waters to leaves in fold on fold,
Now touches this, this long grass in the field:
O under grass, O under grass, the secret.

Surely the seed that stirs beneath this touch
Hears in its ear the wand within the wind,
The miraculous fire from which all years have waned.
This, if it moves, must heal the martyr's wound:
O under grass, O under grass, the secret.

Surely from this the snow-white blood is blown;
Gold marguerite's doom that never comes, comes soon.
Dead saints, white clouds, they stop not near the shrine
But cross the skeleton harp, the unplucked bone:
O under grass, O under grass, the secret.

Ivy entwined about the walls of pride
Clings, where the tales of time in centuried scrawl
Compass the delicate mind, the hand of skill
Touching this fire that never formed a school:
O under grass, O under grass, the secret.

The wired walls hold a castle of desertion.
Already round the gate the nettle springs.
Old, wily murmurs have usurped those songs.
Sheer over this the kestrel ruin hangs:
O under grass, O under grass the secret.

Children pass by for whom a bell has chimed.
Hunters pass by: for these a bell has tolled.
Horns echo backward, but the tower deep-welled
Hangs in the stream with all its woven scroll:
O under grass, O under grass, the secret.

THE MOTHER AND CHILD

Let hands be about him white, O his mother's first,
Who caught him, fallen from light through nine months' haste
Of darkness, hid in the worshipping womb, the chaste
Thought of the creature with its certain thirst.
Looking up to her eyes declined that make her fair
He kicks and strikes for joy, reaching for those dumb springs.
He climbs her, sinks, and his mouth under darkness clings
To the night-surrounded milk in the fire of her hair.

She drops her arm, and, feeling the fruit of his lips,
Tends him cunningly. O, what secrets are set
In the tomb of each breath, where a world of light in eclipse
Of a darkly worshipping world exults in the joy she gave
Knowing that miracle, miracle to beget,
Springs like a star to her milk, is not for the grave.

INFANT NOAH

Calm the boy sleeps, though death is in the clouds.
Smiling he sleeps, and dreams of that tall ship
Moored near the dead stars and the moon in shrouds,
Built out of light, whose faith his hands equip.
It was imagined when remorse of making
Winged the bent, brooding brows of God in doubt.
All distances were narrowed to his waking:
"I built his city, then I cast him out."
Time's great tide falls; under that tide the sands
Turn, and the world is shown there thousand-hilled
To the opening, ageless eyes. On eyelids, hands,
Falls a dove's shade, God's cloud, a velvet leaf.
And his shut eyes hold heaven in their dark sheaf,
In whom the rainbow's covenant is fulfilled.

THE TURNING OF THE LEAVES

Not yet! Do not yet touch,
Break not this branch of silver-birch,
Nor ask the stealthy river why it laves
Black roots that feed the leaves.

Ask first the flickering wren.
He will move further. Ask the rain.
No drop, though round, through that white miracle
Will sink, to be your oracle.

Not yet! Do not yet bend
Close to that root so tightly bound
Loosened by creeping waters as they run
Along the fork's rough groin.

274

Ask not the water yet
Why the root's tapering tendrils eat
Parched earth away that they may be
Nearer the source those fibres must obey.

Behind the bark your hands will find
No Sycorax or flying Daphne faned
And the brown ignorant water bindweed breeds
Not caring there what brows it braids.

Light in the branches weaves.
Hard is the waiting moment while it waves,
This tree whose trunk curves upward from the stream
Where faltering ripples strum.

See how it hangs in air.
The leaves are turning now. We cannot hear
The death and birth of life. But that disguise,
Look up now, softly: break it with your eyes.

Eithne Wilkins

SPOKEN THROUGH GLASS

Here the big stars roll down
like tears
all down your face;
darkness that has no walls, the empty night
that fingers grope for and are lost,
is nightfall in your face.

The big stars roll,
the glittering railway-line unwinds into the constellations.

Over and under you the dark,
in you the rocking night without a foothold,
and no walls, no ceiling,
the parallels that never meet, the pulses winding out to the
    stars.

Night has no end.
Light travelling from the stars is out
before you ride along it
with the black tears falling,
falling,

all fall down.

THE DREAMERS AND THE SEA

(from a cycle, "Parzival")

The dreamers turn;
their shoulders cast, grey mounds, a shadow
on the other side,
still pools of shadow in the retrogressive moon.

Their dreams are in the fern;
their watery dreams
condense.
So while the globe is losing speed
sleep for all is melting of the ice age:
life comes up in the unrolling mist
out of the general sea.

Nor is it enough that man by night
exhales a moister spirit and crawls out from his black body
like a crocodile, towards his mother in that swollen sea.
He has a difficulty of his own
to take breaths deep enough of air:
even by daylight, as he goes about on unrelenting earth,
the serpent
wrings him in the pit and calls him guilty.

COCKCROW

Oh swearing and telling
is a tower falling
that never reaches the ground;
only the rising earth to meet us, and the rising wind.
How fluttering from the fields awash these voices rise,
these cries!
and the idiot pigeons jumping about the stony room,
where so much light is suspended in the gloom
that there is no escape from reading what the message said,
   lifesize,
and recognising everything by name.

This is the tower of rescues that is reached too late.
And what in the topmost storey every time is found
I shall not drink tonight,
but the strong tower floating in the gunmouth, in the flooded
   pool.

For cradled in these cupped and echoing hands
the gunman's head is lolling voiceless, all
its reason gone;

277

and finally the long view
spreading through the skull
into a mere at daybreak, and the drowned cockerels crow.

AND ONLY OUR SHADOW WALKS WITH US

(For Robert Graves)

We who have no perfection but to die
walk among sliding hills and crumpled grassland,
feathery with premonitions of the open sea.
And here some time, when thought hangs as a cloud
motionless between the sun and self turned colourless, a wind
  arises;
then the arm, severe and lonely,
lifts like an apparition, turns the collar up.

We cannot go again to our small house;
nor is it likely we can reach the juggling sea with all its flames.
Inaccurate, fragmentary, shrinking back from traces in the grass,
the earlier footsteps and the patch where others or ourselves
  have lain—
some other century, with lark ascending—we face the wind
blowing backwards from the memory, hair streaming from
  the brow.
For we have no completeness in ourselves, wandering between
  the cold sun and the wind,
wandering between the shadow of our thought,
the shadow, winged, hovering,
and our doom etched out upon that grassland in enormous
  chalk.

Here are bare hills; the curious sheep-track; stones.
We are mere horizon, have no frontiers.
Only the limits of our outstretched arms describe,
in irony of helplessness,
big love or angler's luck.

ANABASIS

(For Edmund Blunden)

There is no sense in asking those who fought—
and that was in another country—
what they suffered, how they got that wound.
Perhaps behind shut eyes they sometimes still experience
the sliding rocks, the gaunt deserted coast, and night
continually falling upon work unfinished and
intolerable weight of arms.
Or tire, without an explanation, of their duty now a servant,
   tireless;
or they lust for some calamity, some bulk
of new compulsion,
secretly they might be glad of war renewed.

Most, if you ask them for a reminiscence,
will not understand.
Only the plain man tells you it was not so bad.
Most have forgotten how it was,
unless in anecdote, fired off a harmless rocket
for the children;
and that reminds them of how far it was, that in the end
   arriving

their arrival did not seem a victory, they had forgotten also
how to be astonished.

None will get an answer from
those who left pain behind them, like an emptied flask
dropped useless in a ditch,
so travelling lighter, lean, with what simplicity of thirst.

And those
for whom the thing is dangerous always,
the struggle still expanding, and the pain old-timer a colossus
at the gate to every sea they enter,
who know too well the battle line is always level with the eyes,
however high they go,
give answer merely: "Oh, we fought."
and to the question whether, then, such things were hard,
confess, laconically:
"Hard."

A HIGH PLACE

They had a pocketful of stories that they told:
how she was partly in another country, brighter than a stone,
and how her mind was an unmanageable field
rough with the shards and tools of other races; by a half-
    buried stream
nettles across the grave-mounds fought the dazzling gorse.

And the headless horseman galloped at full moon.

Even in her height of summer, where no traveller came,
hallucinations floated in her hair transparently, a swarm
    of bees.

And as these things were distantly reported, as a sigh of
  heat on grassland,
the dandelion that has no shame
airily looked through her hilltop eyes.
Nor was there any question if the stories all were true,
hardly acknowledging how shadow mounted from the dale
and whatever mists might hover in her speech, however
  soon night fell.

Only a rumour hinted that the way was difficult to find,
the climbing difficult across forgotten gloomy villages;
and that on this peak, where on clear days one might have
  glimpses of the sea,
no one could say what violence left an outline of uncertain
  skeleton,
of some lost key,
the site of palaces still unexplained,
the vanished columns standing into air, the cloud of bees.

At least she would have gladly in her turn abandoned this,
  flying out
with the huge horseman riding fleshless on the air and out
  of time.
To need no more of the crimson tortuous mouth;
no more of those valleys sunk below the mind; and how,
  aloft, the wild hawks clashed.

PASSAGE OF AN AUGUST

In solitary august, like a story
he met grief's lassie with the quartz-bright hands;
and she became his darling,

281

who was young, was sorry
there among the grasses blowing over pit and brands.

She walked beside him back the way he came,
into the whitening hills, and cut his throat.
Although she called him by another name,
she was no stranger, love. And none
can drive her out.

1938

BARBED WIRE

The silence, with its ragged edge of lost communication,
silence at the latter end,
is now a spiked north wind.

Last words
toss about me in the streets, waste paper
or a cigarette butt in some gutter stream
that overflows
from crumpled darkness.
"Look, I am plunged in the midst of them, a dagger
in their midst."

and over the edge
the nightmares peer, with their tall stories
and the day's unheard-of cry.

1940

FAILURE

What can forgive us for
the clothes left lying and the rocking journey,
flashing poles and pylons standing into fields of air,
in flooded fields?

Something flew out of our hands,
the cup incomplete,
air of invasions and land of defeat.
There was the tree felled in another valley,
behind the flown carpet
and nothing left to remember, all to forgive.

Nothing to remember but
the windows slammed against the cold,
the helmet crushed down on the eyes.

And who, beside the darkened station lamp,
remembering, started back.

1935

SHARK'S FIN

But what dark flag
has thrown a shadow out ahead,
fluttering on chalky ribs?

However far we go,
with our brown eyelids wrinkled
from much looking out, with salty skin and bleaching hair
stiff in the wind, that later dries
above a tideline;

283

whatever exiles and high seas we call our own,
still we can not shake off the whitening wake astern,
the down-pull that would sift us gently, bone from bone;

and how
the lean shadow of another order continually follows,
the unseen jars, the solitary pursuer.

THE EYE

I. THE EYE AS THE DESERT

It is not you that move, but the running sand,
and beyond, those fluid mountains, loaded range of light
up-steepling through the skull.

It is your shadow floating through the bones
taken to be a journey,
or ahead the precipice.
This is the tall shadow dancing where the journey seemed to be
and paints the lips still ghostlier,
brilliant thirst,
the shadow pouring away
in mountains of light, cliffs, staggering waterfalls.

Light curls on your lips
and is the desert in the golden eye.
The shadow, tangled in the imagined journey,
clutched at flashes of the thorn,
while light with its blaze of drums unfolding like a flower
beats round the skull,

284

its trumpets growing longer as the note prolongs the mountains out of reach.

The fingers slip in air, clash with the thornbush and the sand.
The outstretched arms are locked in shadow.

Yet
light splashes
even from the thin plant flowering at your feet, the crying flower
with thorns, whose shadow glides
out of the desert and blots out the sight of hills,
darkens your thirst.

2. THE EYE AS THE COAST

Therefore climb down into this eye
with all its seas,
edge of the sea, grating of pebbles and sharp coast.

This is your beginning, stiff sea-holly,
thistles,
here with your thought hard underfoot and hard in your eye.
This is beginning:
in the small round eye, the staring rock-pool.

Light's centre heaps inside the twisting wave,
the breaking moment is alone, running to light.
Here darkness has solid arms, pulling and pulling down your head,
a stone
with fluttering lashes,

down here among rocks, on a loose wild beach
beside an approaching tide that speaks with your own voice.

Look, among rocks
now wakes the hollow eye, a creeping fire.
And like twilight there arises the person itself,
and you feel this skull
a fragile
burden, a terror
among dreams,
Then the sea-winds ebb from your forehead,
and the clotted hair
streaks the shadowy face like blood:
the body standing with the skin unbroken,
blood with its unburst dams, and bones like towers about
   to fall.

You are your own terror in the dream,
a standstill.
Look! the luminous tall one.

3. THE THIRD EYE

What hands are these upon your thorny shoulders?
what rocks? what knives?

In an empty shell
the roaring of lost mountains roams at large
among the rocks, the desert, and the waves.

VARIATIONS ON A THEME BY SIDNEY KEYES

They said, It will be like snow falling.
And the walls broke down, the soft air crumbled
in our nostrils, flaked to nothingness
between our fingers that were already half asleep.
Then the hills mounted round our heads
like pillows, and the cloudy sky
was drawn up to our chins, there where we lay.

For it was true, and there was snow
falling, marking us out, the shadowy campaigners
who had gone too far and having fallen sick,
scrawled last words in the diary, in the fields of air.
And so we lie half wrapped in snow, with lengthening bones,
where so much light has filled the lantern jaws
and leaves a dark stone in the eye.

Whether it is the wandering of an unseen sun
behind these falling clouds, or only darkness in the flooded
    eye,
we guessed that it might come upon us so; and lie here
under still unwritten sheets, a hatchet pointing
through the drifts of time, this journey
that perhaps we never should have gone
through such snow falling, and so far from help.

George Woodcock

WHITE

White is the evening nature of my thought
When neutral time that drains the night of green
Flows through the dusk in mimic dawn of white.

So pale the distance where blue morning shone
Knits to the whitest crises of our stars,
Burning the nightly ambience of alone,

And evil evident of coloured hours
Dies in this dark, whose sexless shapes of black
Are only active in our twilight fears.

For at day's death the whitest needs awake
When seeping pallor undermines the night
And white submerges all in evening lake,

Where, as a lode attracting all time's light,
You are white's evening nature of my thought.

THE ISLAND

The oars fell from our hands. We climbed the dark
    Slopes of kelp to the stairway up the rock.
Scott went first, grasping the fraying rope.
    The rest of us followed, dragging the iron rack.

The crest was bare, but after scanty search
  In a bird's burrow we found the hunted man.
His flesh was naked and hard as barren earth,
  His arms like scythes. His eyes spoke like a gun.

Before him we retired, unmanned by fear.
  Unarmed, he seemed to move with harmful light.
Scott only stood, shaming us in the end.
  The fugitive surrendered without fight.

We laid him on the painful rack, stretched tight
  His limbs and bound his feet and wrists with wire,
Set leaden weights upon his sunken chest
  And tied his head down by the matted hair.

We turned the cranks and wrenched him hour by hour.
  In silence he endured. He would not speak
Of the hidden ore. At last his joints burst out
  And jetting from the ruptures fire broke.

Then lay before us on the rigid rack
  Straw limbs and a horse's polished skull.
Gulls mocked as walked away across the sea
  The man we hunted but could not keep or kill.

We threw the rack into the hungry surf
  And hacked the turf in anger with our swords.
Then, re-embarking on our fruitless voyage,
  We left the island to the mice and birds.

MERTHYMAWR

Sunday evening. The thick-lipped men binoculared
Steal through the geometric groves of pines,
Observing the steady and fatal hands of poachers
And the young loving in wrinkles of the dunes.

Grey in the wind sand tides against the turrets,
And watchful sight is bridged towards the sea,
Where silent the marram defends a wearing land
And the seagulls climb like Junkers a plaster sky.

The air is alive with voices, the loving whisper,
The rodent screams at neck-constricting hand,
Gulls' earthless wail and dank watchers' laughter.
Always the wind whistles through teeth of sand.

Night falls on the lovers, marram and voices.
Dark hinders eyes, yet aids the brutal hand.
Watchers depart, but the snares are filling.
Wind dries the blood on the moving sand.

IMAGINE THE SOUTH

Imagine the South from which these migrants fled,
Dark-eyed, pursued by arrows, crowned with blood,
Imagine the stiff stone houses and the ships
Blessed with wine and salt, the quivering tips
Of spears and edges signalling in the sun
From swords unscabbarded and sunk in brine,
Imagine the cyclamen faces and yielding breasts
Hungered after in a dead desert of icy mists,

Imagine, for though oblivious, you too are cast
Exile upon a strange and angry coast.

Going into exile away from youth,
You too are losing a country in the south,
Losing, in the red daylight of a new shore
Where you are hemmed by solitude and fear,
The loving faces far over a sea of time,
The solid comfort and the humane dream
Of a peaceful sky, the consoling patronage
And the golden ladder to an easy age,
All these are lost, for you too have gone away
From your Southern home upon a bitter journey.

There is no home for you marked on the compass.
I see no Penelope at the end of your Odysseys,
And all the magic islands will let you down.
Do not touch the peaches and do not drink the wine,
For the Dead Sea spell will follow all you do,
And do not talk of tomorrow, for to you
There will only be yesterday, only the fading land,
The boats on the shore and tamarisks in the sand
Where the beautiful faces wait, and the faithful friends.
They will people your mind. You will never touch
  their hands.

SONNET

Looking into the windows that doom has broken
Where the vague star illumines death and dust
And the shadows of actions whose ends are forsaken
Stir under the falling walls, senile and lost,

And looking into the doorways where unspoken names
Shine and disintegrate on the rotting plaques,
Surviving their owners who have left like dreams,
Sinking into the past as sea-sucked wrecks,

Remember, stranger, that here men grew and worked,
Loved and were angry, and in general lived
Peaceable lives till one day, spitted on their brothers' knives,
Stuck to the curdling heart by nails they loved,
They died in horror and their towns were left,
And rotted, buried under the dust and leaves.

TREE FELLING

The bright axe breaks the silence in the wood,
The ivory chips spray over crushed nettles,
And the red slender pine sways and totters
Shuddering its boughs in the chill of death.

All down the hill the yellow teeth of stumps
Stud the tramped moss and broken willow herb;
The piled long bolls point northward to the Pole,
Their fragrant lymph seeping from broken veins.

Borne away in the blue wake of tractors,
The lopped trees leave for ever their fitting landscape;
They will grow again in the underground valleys
Where the black miners creep beneath a sagging sky.

And here the ploughs will traverse, as in Carthage
Marking the end of a kingdom, the day of the squirrel
And the blue jay shattering along the mossed valleys
Between the still pines. The silence of felted needles

Breeding its ugly toadstools and sick brown orchids,
Has ended its seeming permanence. Cyclic transition
Will reign on the hillside, with its bare and ice-baked winters,
And its multitudinous summer under the whispering corn.

POEM FROM LONDON, 1941.

The fading whistles outline our broken city
Against the dead chart and distant zodiac,
Against the decaying roads, empty and perilous,
That join our exile with the land we seek.
Kissed onward by the pistol, we all are exile,

Expatriate, wandering in the illusive streets
Of faked identity, which swing towards a past
That is no Indies regained by circuitous sea routes.

The bridges are down, the visas are invalid;
We cannot turn on our tracks away from fate.
I stand at the 'phone and listen in to death,
And dare not stuff my ears and ring off hate.

Yet I behold an angel like a falcon
Bearing a speaking flame across the dark
To sing in the dumb streets of cretin children
For the silly hearts that cannot even break.

And under the windows of a drunken pub
A man sits, listening, like a wind-squat tree,
Unnamed, his face a map of paper, his bone hands
Moulding from the burning voice a phoenix day.

SUNDAY ON HAMPSTEAD HEATH

Underfoot on the hill the water spurts
Thickly out of the brilliant matted grasses
Where the slopes fold in groins and thighs of earth
And the winter sunlight in thin golden masses
Falls through the lunging wind that swings the skirts
Of the girls walking with their soldiers over the heath.

A group of dwarf fir trees marks the crest
With boughs like drowners' hands that claw the sky.
Far down the slope a white springboard rears
Its gaunt and skeleton frame above the grey
Tossed pool where in summer the divers raced
But where now only the ducks bob, resting their oars.

Leaning their weight on London, the smoky roofs
Below the hill stretch out their infinite folds,
A stony sea, far in miasmic depth
Where men sleep out their empty dreams of deeds,
And towers and domes, surging like green reefs,
Rise up heroic and powerful in their sloth.

Here on the hilltop my friends and I sit down.
They talk of prison; the conversation falls
And I say, "One evening we must drink at the Spaniard's."
I do not know what they are thinking as their heels
Kick out the turf and their gaze creeps over the scene,
Peering through the smoke for the customary landmarks.

But, going away in my mind from their shut faces,
Away from the quiet hilltop and the leisurely men
Digging their new gardens below in the little valley,

I enter the forest of rooftops and, under the grimy stone,
Walk among the pipedreams of men in braces
Reading in Sunday newspapers the end of faith and folly.

And in the broken slums see the benign lay down
Their empty, useless love, and the stunted creep,
Ungainly and ugly, towards a world more great
Than the moneyed hopes of masters can ever shape.
In the dead, grey streets I hear the women complain
And their voice is a spark to burn the myth of the state.

And here where my friends talk and the green leaves spurt
Quietly from waterlogged earth, and the dry twigs bud,
I see a world will rise more lovely than Blake
Knew in his winged dreams, and the leaves of good
Will burst on branches dead from winter's hurt,
When the broken rise and the silent voices speak.

David Wright

WALKING TO DEDHAM

(To Kristin)

Lean your small head against the Spring,
That what's abundant of the year
May be promised by the plum
Orchards which all together seem to wear
The frock of winter; lean
Your face toward the forehead of the year,
To the fresh fields pebbled with many flowers,
Scattered upon a Summer's littoral.

295

Landscape and region of a dream,
Seen from a visionary hill
Between two seasons Spring
And Summer, when the world becoming real,
Its obverse face of pain,
Of death, and of indifference to ill,
Slowly unveils; but at this season
Dazzles the skeleton with thick petals.

What winds there, and what flowers blow
Over the acreage of peace,
Streams that through orchards flow,
Bowed with their bloom as heavy as a fleece,
The frank of winter, now
Surround you in the central folds of peace
No certain hurt of the hovering hours
Or grief may pierce, or falling, seem to fall.

John Bate

COLOGNE

To-day my heart is heavy
with the sorrows of Cologne,
the city reaps the bitter
harvest its enemies have sown,
and I, that enemy, am
consumed with their bitterness.

How can the June sun shine
adding its pitiful glory

to the cruel glare of the flames,
casting shadows with a jagged line,
this page of the city's story
lighting, which is dark with shames.

The dry confetti blossoms
in this village street, where tramp
off-duty airmen, lie like the sun's
small, coloured tears, and here
where Cologne is a word city,
articulated in the cultured drone
of radio announcers, thinking
they have news to match the gospel,
but sounding in their voice no pity,
our hardened, revengeful will,
of which mine is a part, will suffer,
for the victor cities always discover,
unaware of it before it grows,
the interacting sorrow of their foes.

June 1942.

Audrey Beecham

EXILE

A wind like this tonight
For such a one:
To clutch his throat
And bind with ice-thongs tight.

297

A shower of pointed stones
To cover him
Where he may fall
A pall to grind his bones.

Or he one night be shown
An empty town,
In endless rain
To wander there alone:

And pass the churchyard wall
And see inside
The long-extended arms
Of the dead, stretched wide.

George Bruce

KINNAIRD HEAD

I go North to cold, to home, to Kinnaird,
Fit monument for our time.
This is the outermost edge of Buchan.
Inland the sea birds range,
The tree's leaf has salt upon it,
The tree turns to the low stone wall.
And here a promontory rises towards Norway,
Irregular to the top of thin grey grass
Where the spindrift in storm lays its beads.
The water plugs in the cliff sides,
The gull cries from the clouds
This is the consummation of the plain.

O impregnable and very ancient rock,
Rejecting the violence of water,
Ignoring its accumulations and strategy,
You yield to history nothing.

Francis Douglas Davison

BOUGHT

Fine rays of praise my asking rings from her
rose and the dying warrior can do no more
at night on frosty plains
to satisfy the heart's desire
creation's bloom on dying things admire
the fire down empty corridors the black night makes
incarnate in the strength that sleeps it
so dies like days in emblems pressed
on mortal thoughts and fears which follow them
if pity finds a heart and fills the hunger.
Her nature drawn in smiles
not merely wished or guessed
miles after hours I strove to hold the essence frozen
only she dimmed and gave my gaze to remember
empty hands on the counter fold, unfold
in thoughts' weave rest unrest.

James Kirkup

MORTALLY

The garden cannot move.
The terraces are sunken
invisibly in snow
the balustrades are there
whoever leans on them will fall into the bay
open the windows and the flowers
will disappear ·or else
geraniums alone remain.

The lawns at evening bifurcate
and grow into a woman with a grass
grave for the outline of her body.

The dead that lay along the branches of an orchard
creep into the season's river
and the ruin.

LA BETE HUMAINE

The trains of thought
meet generally speaking
bifurcation revelation
Soupault said and Zola never saw...

'les mecaniciens des locomotives ont des yeux blancs'

and wrote it in his head.
Certainly the enginedrivers
or the ones I mean have statuary eyes.
They show them to you sometimes at a terminus.

Paul Potts

JEAN

There is a wild flower growing
Inside a broken vase,
On a mantle in my memory.

This flower will die
When you are dead,
And while you live will grow.

Because each petal and its stem
Is like long years, of waiting and of hope,
So useless and so void.

Julian Orde

THE CHANGING WIND

Past my window runs a tree,
All the leaves are in my room,
A shiver of water passes over.
There is no stillness ever again.
I saw the table break in three,
I saw the walls cascading down,
I saw the hard hair of my lover
Drift out upon the flowing green.
I saw the clove dark enemy

Stare from the bed where I had lain,
I saw my face in hers to be.
There is no stillness ever again.

Sun and wind had come for me—
What is my house but a flight of wings?
A flight of leaves, a flutter of rain,
A sidelong slipping of light in rings?

And now a scream possesses me—
Too high to hear, yet can I hear it;
And now transfixed upon a pain,
Too thin to feel yet must I bear it—
This scream, this pain, they are not mine,
Water and air is all I am,
A tree has shaken the staircase down—
Then what has rustled and entered in?

I knew the other ones had come.
I knew my heart was theirs to claim.
I felt the millions in my room.
There is no being alone again.

BIOGRAPHICAL NOTES

LOUIS ADEANE was born in 1922, and his education was "self-imposed." He is an anarcho-pacifist and was a Conscientious Objector in World War II. He has worked at a wide variety of jobs, and has published articles and poems in *Now* and numerous other magazines. He has published one book of verse, *The Night Loves Us*.

KENNETH ALLOTT is a lecturer in English Literature at Liverpool University. He was born in 1912, educated at Durham and Oxford, and has worked as a journalist, schoolmaster and tutor. He is married and has two children. He has published three books, *Poems, The Ventriloquist's Doll* (poems) and *Jules Verne*, a biography. He is now at work on a study of Matthew Arnold.

GEORGE BARKER was born in 1913 and was educated at Marlborough Public School. He is one of the founders of the contemporary Romantic movement, and has published two books of prose and seven of verse. In the United States he is published by The Macmillan Company, except for his *Sacred and Secular Elegies* with New Directions.

JOHN BATE is a young Catholic poet and is editor of *Leaven*. He was educated in Birmingham, and during the War was a pacifist and worked in a Bomb Disposal Squad. He has published little, lives on a farm, and is married.

JOHN BAYLISS was born in 1919. While at Cambridge he was literary editor of the *Granta*. He served in the RAF during the War. He has published two books of verse and a novel.

AUDREY BEECHAM is a niece of the conductor. She was educated at Oxford, where she now lives.

ALISON BOODSON is now a physician at University College Hospital, London. She was born in 1925, and received the "usual English liberal education." Her first poems were written at the age of sixteen and published in *Poetry London*.

GEORGE BRUCE is a Scottish poet. He was born in 1909, lives in Buchan, and has published one book, *Sea Talk*.

BRENDA CHAMBERLAIN lives in Wales, where she was born. She studied painting at the Royal Academy School. She works at her painting and writing on an island off the Welsh coast or in a mountain cottage on the mainland. She is a skier and mountaineer.

ALEX COMFORT was born in London in 1920, and educated at Highgate School and Trinity College, Cambridge. A physician, he is now engaged in private practice, research and lecturing in physiology at the London Hospital. He is the author of several books of prose and verse, two of which, *The Power House*, a novel, and *Song of Lazarus*, poems, have been

305

published in the United States by The Viking Press. His most recent work is *The Novel and Our Time*.

FRANCIS DOUGLAS DAVISON was born in 1919 and educated at Cambridge. He has lived much in France, and his work was represented in *Atlantic Antology*.

KEITH DOUGLAS was born in 1920 and educated at Christ's Hospital (a public School) and Oxford. He was killed in Normandy. Since his death *Poetry London* has published two books, *Alamein to Zem-Zem*, and *Bête Noire*.

ADAM DRINAN is a Scottish poet. He has published four books of verse, *Men of the Rocks*, *Ghosts of the Strath*, *Women of the Happy Isle* and *The Macphails of London*.

LAWRENCE DURRELL was born in 1912 and educated at St. Edmund's School in Canterbury. He settled in Corfu but was driven out by the War, after which he worked for the British Ministry of Information in Alexandria and later in Rhodes. He returned to England in 1947. He has published several books including *The Black Book* and *Prospero's Cell*. While in Egypt during the War, he edited the magazine and anthology *Personal Landscape*. In the United States he was published by Reynal and Hitchcock, and *The Black Book* is announced by Circle.

PATRICK EVANS was born in 1913 and educated at Oxford. During the War he served in the Tank Corps and also as a parachutist. He lived in Greece for four years, is married, and a book of his verse is about to be published by *Poetry London*.

GAVIN EWART served in the Army during the War. He was born in 1914 and was educated at Wellington and Cambridge. He has published one book of verse.

G. S. FRASER was born in 1915 in Scotland. He served as a Sergeant-Major in the British Army during the War. He has published two books of verse and has also translated Patrice de la Tour du Pin's *La Vie Récluse en Poésie*. He has written a book about South America soon to be published by The Harvill Press, and has translated poems of Neruda.

ROY FULLER is a lawyer with a practice in London. He was born in 1912, is married and has one child. During the War he served in the Royal Navy. He has published two books of verse.

WREY GARDINER was born in Plymouth in 1901. He is an editor of *Poetry Quarterly* and chairman of Grey Walls Press. He has published several books, including *The Gates of Silence* and *The Dark Thorn*.

ROBERT GARIOCH, born in 1909, is a Scottish poet. He has published one book, *17 Poems for Sixpence*.

DAVID GASCOYNE is now living in Paris, and was one of the first English poets to be influenced by Surrealism. He was born in 1916. He is the author of *Opening Day, A Short Survey of Surrealism, Man's Life is This Meat, Hoelderlin Poems 1937-42,* published by *Poetry London.*

W. S. GRAHAM was born in 1917. He is one of the youngest and most independent Scottish poets. During the War he worked as an engineer in England. In 1947 he won an Atlantic Award in Literature, and last year he came to America and taught at New York University. He is the author of *Seven Journeys, 2nd Poems,* and *Cage Without Grievance.*

JOHN HEATH-STUBBS was born in London in 1918, and was educated at Queens College, Oxford. He has published four books, including a translation of the poems of Leopardi, with New Directions. His poems will be published in the United States by William Sloane.

J. F. HENDRY is now in Vienna as a member of the British Control Commission. He was born in Glasgow in 1912. He was one of the founders of Apocalypse, and edited the Apocalyptic anthology *The White Horseman* with Henry Treece. He has published two books of verse, and has long been active in the Scottish Renascence.

RAYNER HEPPENSTALL is now a feature producer at the BBC. He was born in 1911 in Yorkshire, and was educated there and in France. He spent four and a half years in the Army during the War. He is married and has two children. He has published three books of poems, now gathered in *Collected Poems,* two novels, *The Blaze of Noon* and *Saturnine,* and two books of criticism, *Apology for Dancing* and *The Double Image.*

NIGEL HESELTINE was born in 1916 in North Wales. He is now a medical student in Dublin, and is also studying psychoanalysis and criminology. Formerly he worked in the theater and as a journalist. He has published two volumes of verse, a travel book on Albania, translations of Welsh poetry, a book of short stories, and a translation of Buchner's *Wozzek.*

SEAN JENNETT was born in 1912. He began writing at the age of six, and printed his own works at eight, and has been a writer and printer or publisher ever since. He is now a director and designer for Grey Walls and Falcon Presses. He has published a book on typography, and two books of verse, *Always Adam* and *The Cloth of Flesh.*

GLYN JONES is a schoolteacher in South Wales. During the War he was a Conscientious Objector. He has published one book, *Poems.*

SIDNEY KEYES was born in 1922 and was killed in Tunisia in 1942. He was educated at Oxford. Before he died he had published one book, *Collected Poems.* He is published in America by Henry Holt & Company.

JAMES KIRKUP is a schoolteacher. Before the War he lived for many years in France. During the War he worked on the land as a Conscientious

Objector. He has done a considerable amount of translation from the French and is at present engaged in translating Pierre Jean Jouve.

LAURIE LEE was born in 1914, and spent some years in Spain before the Civil War. He has recently been published in New York by Doubleday & Company.

DENISE LEVERTOV was born in 1923. Her father is a Russian Jew who became an Anglican theologian; her mother is Welsh. She studied Russian ballet from the age of twelve to sixteen. During the War she served for four years as a hospital nurse, and she has worked in various odd jobs such as land girl, charwoman, children's nurse and companion to an alcoholic. She has published one book of verse, *The Double Image*. She recently married an American G. I. and hopes to come to the States.

ALUN LEWIS was born in Wales in 1915 and died in Burma in 1944. He published two books of verse, *Raider's Dawn* and *Ha! Ha! Amongst the Trumpets*, and one of short stories, *The Last Inspection*. He is published by Macmillan in the United States.

EMANUEL LITVINOV states that he is no relation to the late, or mislaid, Maxim. He was born in 1915 and went to school "until fourteen but for all purposes uneducated." He spent six years in the British Army, is married and has one daughter. He has published two books, *The Untried Soldier* and *A Crown for Cain*.

NORMAN McCAIG teaches school in Scotland. He was born in 1910. He has published two books of verse, *Far Cry* and *The Inward Eye*.

HUGH MACDIARMID (Christopher Murray Grieve) was born in Scotland in 1892. He was educated at Edinburgh University and served in World War I as a non-combatant in the Medical Corps. With R. B. Cunningham-Graham and Compton Mackenzie he founded the Scottish Nationalist Party, from which he was later expelled as a Communist. He was then expelled from the Communist Party for his Scottish Nationalism. He is the leader of the revival of serious verse in the Scottish vernacular, and has published many books of verse, one, recently, with Contemporary Poetry in Baltimore.

SORLEY MACLEAN (in Gaelic, Somhairle MacGhill Eathain, pronounced Sorley Maclean) is one of the best poets of the Gaelic Revival. He has published one book of verse, *Dain do Eimhir*.

JOSEPH GORDON MACLEOD was born in 1903. He was educated at an English Public School and University, and was called to the Bar but never practiced. He has worked as book reviewer, private tutor, actor, play producer, director, and from 1938 to 1945 as one of the best known BBC broadcasters. He has recently been touring Russia to study the Russian theater. He has published books of verse, criticism, fiction and autobiography, and has written plays and films.

CHARLES MADGE was born in Johannesburg in 1912 and was educated at Winchester and Magdalen College, Oxford. With Tom Harrison he founded Mass Observation, a sociological research movement. He once worked as a journalist and is now an editor of Pilot Press.

OS MARRON was a young miner who died in 1946 of tuberculosis. Shortly before his death he was discovered and encouraged by Alex Comfort. His poems have appeared in *Poetry Folios* and *Poetry Quarterly*.

WILLIAM MONTGOMERIE is a schoolteacher. He was born in 1904, is married, and as well as verse, writes short stories and criticism. He has just completed a study of *Hamlet*.

NICHOLAS MOORE is the son of the philosopher G. E. Moore. He was born in 1918 and educated at Cambridge. He is married and has one daughter. He now works as a publisher and has edited a selection of American short stories. He is a prolific writer and has published several books of verse, two with *Poetry London*.

DOUGLAS NEWTON was a Conscientious Objector during the War and worked on the land in Cambridgeshire. Since the War he has Worked in publishers' offices.

NORMAN NICHOLSON was born at Millom, Cumberland, in 1914, and still lives there. He lectures for the Workers' Educational Association in the mining towns of Cumberland. In the United States he is published by Dutton's.

JULIAN ORDE was born in 1919 and grew up in Paris and Chelsea. She was on the stage for six years, but now writes for films and radio.

PAUL POTTS is Canadian by birth. He was educated at Stowe (England) and spent much of his youth in Italy. He has published much of his own work on broadsheets which he used to sell on the streets. During the War he served in the Army Education Corps. He has published one book of verse, *Instead of a Sonnet*, is working on a study of Silone, and has written his autobiography, which will soon be published.

F. T. PRINCE is published in London by Faber & Faber, and in New York by New Directions.

KATHLEEN RAINE was born in 1908 and raised in Northumberland and London. She took a degree at Cambridge in Natural Sciences. In 1944 she was received into the Roman Catholic Church. She has published two books of verse, *Stone and Flower* and *Living in Time* (Poetry London).

HENRY REED is a critic, who has written notably on T. S. Eliot. His book of verse, *A Map of Verona*, is published in America by Reynal & Hitchcock.

KEIDRYCH RHYS is one of the leaders of the Welsh Renascence. He is the son of a Welsh farmer. During the War he served as an anti-aircraft gunner, but was invalided and went to work at the Ministry of Information. He is the editor of *Wales*.

ANNE RIDLER was once secretary to T. S. Eliot. She was born in 1912, is married and has two daughters. She has published three books of verse and edited the *Little Book of Modern Verse* (Faber).

LYNETTE ROBERTS was born in Buenos Aires of Welsh parents and educated in French and Spanish convents. She is married to Keidrych Rhys.

W. R. RODGERS was born in 1909 in Northern Ireland. For twelve years he was a country parson in Ireland, and he is now with the BBC. He has published one book of verse, *Awake*, which also appeared in the United States, with Harcourt Brace & Co.

D. S. SAVAGE was born in 1917 of "lower middle class parents." He worked for several years at an assortment of ill-paid jobs, is married and has four children. During the War he was a Conscientious Objector. He now lives in Cornwall where he and his wife run a guest house. He has published two books of verse and one of criticism.

FRANCIS SCARFE was born in 1911 and educated at Durham University, Cambridge and the Sorbonne. He worked as Supervisor in French at Trinity College, Cambridge, and as Assistant at the Collège Chaptal, Paris. During the War he served in the Army. He is the author of *Appassionata* (poems), and *Auden and After* (criticism), and has also translated *Les Chants de Maldoror* and Pierre Emmanuel's poems for *Poetry London*.

SIDNEY GOODSIR SMITH was born in 1915 in Scotland. One of the most interesting of the younger poets writing in Doric, he has published three books of verse, *Skail Wind*, *The Wanderer* and *The Deevil's Waltz*.

WILLIAM SOUTAR was born in 1898. Soon after taking his M. A. at Edinburgh University he became paralyzed and spent the rest of his life bedridden, hardly able to move. His bedroom, with a great window overlooking a garden, was equipped with various devices to make it possible for him to live and work and read. Before his death in 1943 he wrote an immense mass of poetry, now reduced to one volume, *Selected Poems*.

BERNARD SPENCER works with The British Council in Turin. He was assistent editor of *New Verse*, and during the War lectured at Juad University in Cairo. His book *Aegean Islands* has just been published in New York by Doubleday.

STEPHEN SPENDER has been teaching at Sarah Lawrence College, near New York. He was born in 1909, and educated at Oxford. Before the War he spent several years in Germany, an experience which considerably influenced his work. He is married and has one child — a son. In the United States he is published by Random House.

DEREK STANFORD was born in 1918 and educated at Latymer. During the War he worked on the land as a Conscientious Objector. He has published two books, *A Romantic Miscellany* (verse, with John Bayliss), and *The Freedom of Poetry* (anthology). With David West he edits the magazine *Resistance*, and he is at work on a translation of Apollinaire, a collection of modern French poetry, and a new book of poems.

JULIAN SYMONS is now working as a copy writer for an advertising agency and is writing a biography of his brother, A. J. A. Symons. He was born in 1912; during the War he served in the Royal Armoured Corps. He is the author of two books of verse, and the founder and editor of *Twentieth Century Verse*, one of the liveliest verse magazines of the 1930's. He has written two excellent detective novels, is an enthusiastic sportsman, and a critic of considerable importance.

DYLAN THOMAS was born in Wales in 1914, and educated at the Swansea Grammar School. He is the subject of a book by Henry Treece, soon to be published in London by Lindsay Drummond, and probably distributed in America by New Directions. His own first book of poems was called *18 Poems*, published by The Parton Press. Later came *The Map of Love* which included both stories and verse, *Portrait of The Artist As a Young Dog* (autobiographical stories, in print, with New Directions) and most recently, *Deaths & Entrances*. His American volumes, *The World I Breathe* and *New Poems* are now out of print, but New Directions has re-issued the bulk of their contents in its *Selected Writings* of Dylan Thomas volume, with introduction by J. R. Sweeney. Thomas worked at a number of jobs until he became interested in radio broadcasting and acting. He has a fine voice and is a remarkable reader of poetry, attracting much attention with his BBC programs. He has been working recently on a novel, and writing films scripts.

TERENCE TILLER now works in the Features Department of the BBC. He was born in Cornwall in 1916 and educated at Cambridge. He has lectured at Fuad University, Egypt, and at Cambridge. He is married and has one daughter.

RUTHVEN TODD is now living in the United States. He was born in Scotland in 1914. He has worked at various jobs and was in the ARP during the War. He has published three books of poems, two novels, a book of essays, and has edited Gilchrist's *Life of Blake*.

HENRY TREECE is married, lives in Lincolnshire and breeds Old English sheep dogs. His *Collected Poems*, gathering the work of four previous volumes, were recently published in the United States by Alfred Knopf. He has also written *How I See Apocalypse* (essays), and *Epilogue to Death* (short stories) and a book on Dylan Thomas. With Stephan Schimanski he edits the personalist bi-yearly *Transformation*. In the War he served as a Flight Lieutenant in the RAF.

JOHN WALLER was born in 1917 at Oxford. He was educated at Weymouth College and Worcester College, Oxford, and edited the Oxford-Cambridge review, *Fords and Bridges*. Later he founded the literary quarterly *Kingdom Come*, one of the most influential periodicals of the first expression of the new Romanticism. He served as a Captain with the British Army in the Middle East during the War.

VERNON WATKINS was born in Wales in 1906, and still lives there. He has published two books of verse, *The Ballad of Mari Lllwyd* and *The Lamp and the Veil*. A collection of his poems has recently been published in the United States by New Directions. He is a banker.

EITHNE WILKINS was educated at Oxford. Her first poems appeared there just before the War, and in Roger Roughton's magazine *Contemporary Poetry*. She has since worked in publishing houses and as a translator.

GEORGE WOODCOCK is one of the editors of *Freedom* and the founder and editor of *Now*. He has published two books of verse, *The White Island* and *The Centre Cannot Hold* and also a biography of *William Godwin*, a study of *Aphra Behn*, and a book on anarchism, *Anarchy or Chaos*. He has also written several pamphlets on housing, agriculture, railways, ethics, and other questions.

DAVID WRIGHT was born in South Africa in 1920 and at the age of seven became totally deaf. He was educated in South Africa and at Oriel College, Oxford. He is now working as a journalist.

NOTE

The most notable omission from this collection is the poet, Edwin Muir. He has been left out of the Scottish collection because he does not write in Scots and considers himself independent of the Scots Renascence. He is older than the poets writing in English who have been included in this volume, and moreover he is well represented in several available anthologies.

GLOSSARY FOR PAGE 74

(ghaisties - ghosts; airms - arms; mell - mix; timm - empty; ayont - beyond; glunch - sneer; reek - smoke; creeshy - greasy; swat - sweat; grup - grip; alowe - below; loups - leaps; howe - hollow; wame - womb; sonsie - jolly; "The flesh be bruckle and the fiends be slee" - a quotation from Dunbar's *Timor Mortis Conturbat Me*; pree - prove; dree - dwindle; lauch - laugh.)

Date Due

It
Bec

NOV 1 '58